PARSON GRAY

TRADE QUILTS

PARSON GRAY

TRADE QUILTS

20 ROUGH-HEWN PROJECTS

David Butler

CHRONICLE BOOKS

SAN FRANCISCO

Library of Congress Cataloging-in-Publication Data

Names: Butler, David, 1965- author. | Guzman, Susan, illustrator.
Title: Parson Gray trade quilts : 20 rough-hewn projects
  / David Butler ; illustrations and patterns by Susan Guzman.
Description: San Francisco, California : Chronicle Books, LLC,
[2016] |
  Includes index.
Identifiers: LCCN 2016006102 | ISBN 9781452134482 (hardcover
: alk. paper)
Subjects: LCSH: Patchwork quilts. | Patchwork—Patterns. |
Americana in art.
Classification: LCC TT835 .B8935 2016 | DDC 746.46—dc23 LC
record available at https://lccn.loc.gov/2016006102

Manufactured in China

Illustrations and patterns by Susan Guzman
Designed and typeset by TO/GO/TK

10 9 8 7 6 5 4 3 2 1

Chronicle books and gifts are available at special quantity
discounts to corporations, professional associations, literacy
programs, and other organizations. For details and discount
information, please contact our corporate/premiums department
at corporatesales@chroniclebooks.com or at 1-800-759-0190.

Chronicle Books LLC
680 Second Street
San Francisco, California 94107
www.chroniclebooks.com

CONTENTS

INTRODUCTION 7

NOTES FOR ALL PROJECTS 8

BASIC TOOLS 9

FABRICS 11

   Canvas 12

   Cotton 12

   Denim 12

   Linen 12

   Wool 12

   Vintage Fabrics 13

GRITTY TECHNIQUES
FOR GORGEOUS TEXTURE 13

   Distressing Fabric 13

   Staining, Fading, and Dyeing Fabric 16

   Coffee and Tea Staining 17

   Fading Fabric 18

   Natural Staining 18

   Fabric Dyeing and Paint Staining 19

QUILT-MAKING STEPS 21

   Prep for Quilting 22

   Layering a Quilt Sandwich 22

   Basting Methods 23

   Quilting Methods 24

   Finishing the Quilt Edges 26

   Appliqué Stitching 31

   Embroidery Stitches 32

THE QUILTS 35

   Navajo Blanket Quilt 37

   Grainery Quilt 41

   Iron Bars Quilt 47

   Forged Block Quilt 51

   Maritime Quilt 55

   Horse Blanket Quilt 63

   Old Glory Quilt 69

   Fort Battery Quilt 75

   1890s Trader's Quilt 83

   Bear Paw Quilt 89

   World's Fair Quilt 95

   Skeleton Crew Quilt 103

   Painted Desert Quilt 109

   Coal Mine Quilt 119

   Falling Wind Quilt 125

   English Cross Quilt 133

   Southwest Passage Quilt 141

   Bull's-Eye Quilt 147

   Carpetbagger Quilt 153

   Arrow Quilt 159

GLOSSARY 164

INDEX 166

INTRODUCTION

I started out in the quilting world very much behind the scenes, as the husband and graphic artist for Amy Butler, print and sewing pattern designer extraordinaire. You've probably heard of her. Me? Well . . .

They've let me creep around backstage in the fabric design and quilting industry for many years now, lifting heavy boxes, shaking hands, and having the right tools to help out where I was needed. All the while, I was absorbing the craft, the passion, and collecting the wherewithal to do something of my own. Thanks to the coaxing of my beloved Amy, and the support of my friends at FreeSpirit, I came out with my own line of fabrics, focusing on "guy-friendly" designs in richly muted dark tones. My personal taste leans toward mid-century modern, Japanese shibori, and American folk art, with a dash of rock and roll. As it turns out, there's an audience for that, and it's not just guys. As my fabrics have grown, so has my penchant for using them. Please understand, I'm actually a pretty lousy sewer. I can do it, but it's not a skill I've had time to hone, and I realize that many other folks may feel the same way. They want to create, but they're intimidated by the process. That's how the idea for *Parson Gray Trade Quilts* came into being. I wanted to create a new design paradigm that celebrates reckless artistic abandon, for those of us not seeking perfection, but empowering curiosity. There will be mistakes, and that's totally fine. In fact, that's part of the story and part of the magic that happens when you shake off the constraints of making everything just so. In the world of quilting, which I admire and love, this is equal to coloring way outside the lines.

By taking on this daunting idea of a quilt book for the uninitiated, I had a conundrum on my hands: I do not write sewing patterns or instructions. Amy does, but she's way too busy with her own! So I turned to the only person I could think of who is a masterful sewing-pattern writer, and also someone with enough creative allowance to understand what the heck I was trying to do. Susan Guzman has been a friend for years, and she jumped at the idea of co-creating a new way of looking at sewing and quilts. She was able to break away from her ingrained amazing skills, step back, and interpret the rantings of a lunatic-deconstructionist graphic artist. As it turns out, telling people how to make something imperfect is about as hard as telling them how to make it as perfect as they possibly can. At least there's a formula for the latter.

So here's the gist of this book. It's a guide of rustic sewing ideas for modern pioneers. Yes, there are patterns, and yes, there are instructions, but more importantly, there are ideas. Ideas for coloring outside the lines, embracing patina, reveling in whoops, and blending vintage with modern, as I love to do with my fabric-print designs. Creating lived-in is a part of the goal, as is getting funky with it, and maybe even a little dirty. It's not perfectly square?!? Yeah, I know. Cool, right?

NOTES FOR ALL PROJECTS

○ Please read through all instructions before beginning a project.

○ Unless otherwise noted, all fabric yardage given is
based on 42" to 44" [107 to 112 cm] wide fabric
from the bolt.

○ Prep fabric: Prewash new cotton, polyester, or
blended fabrics in your washing machine using
warm water to remove the sizing the manufacturer uses in the printing process; tumble dry,
low heat. Gently preshrink wool fabric and wash
any natural fiber vintage fabrics by hand using
cold water; hang or dry flat. Press out any wrinkles from washed fabrics before using. Tip: Make
small diagonal clips in the corners of each fabric
piece before washing to help prevent fraying and
tangling.

○ Use ¼" [6 mm] seam allowances unless otherwise stated.

BASIC TOOLS

These tools are used for all of the projects in this book. They are the essential supplies quilters should have in their sewing "arsenal." Any additional notions or other items you may need for a project will be noted in its specific instructions.

- Sewing machine
- Extra sewing-machine needles
- Assortment of hand-sewing needles
- Iron and ironing board
- Large box of quilter's safety pins (optional)
- 6" x 24" [15 x 61 cm] acrylic ruler
- Rotary cutter and 24" x 36" [61 x 91 cm] mat
- Scissors, both large and small pair
- Fabric marking pencil and/or fabric marker
- Straight pins
- Quilter's clips (optional)

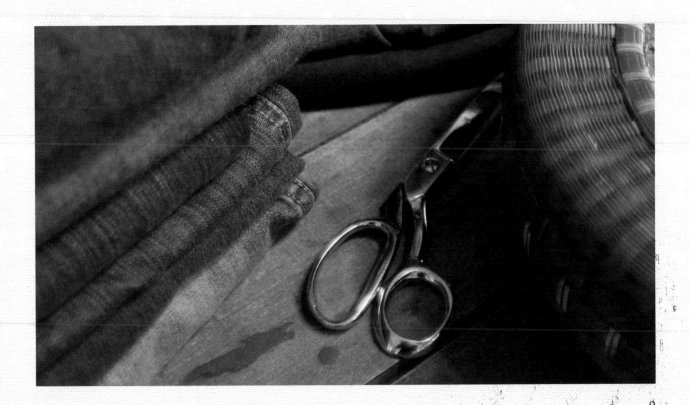

FABRICS

Approach your choice of fabrics with a quest for adventure and a sense of humor. Why? Well, vintage fabrics present their own inherent patina and charm, but in combining them with newer fabrics, you'll need to have a little patience and forethought. The same goes for combining different types of fabric, i.e., cotton with wool, wool with denim, and so on. There may be a need to change needles for heavier-weight fabrics, address the speed of your stitch, or change the weight of the thread for lighter-weight fabrics. There are dozens of great websites that give guidance for practically any sewing question. A couple of my favorites are www.thesewingdirectory.co.uk and www.threadsmagazine.com.

I didn't work with voiles, silk, or other fashion fabrics in this book. For the styles of these quilts, I felt it necessary to start with some of the easier-to-work-with, more utilitarian fabrics, as each fabric brings its own set of demands. With that in mind, I can give you a synopsis of the basic fabrics that are covered in this book.

CANVAS

Canvas is the heavy-duty workhorse of cotton fabrics. It has a plain weave that is very sturdy, yet is easy to sew with a durable needle (size 100/16 to 110/18, depending on the type of thread being used) and a stitch length setting of 3.0 to 4.0. Go slow and steady; don't jerk the fabric through your machine. New canvas can be quite stiff and it will shrink some, so washing in advance is always a good idea. Keep in mind that open edges will fray like crazy, as the weave is simple and opens up quickly. Consider sewing a zigzag stitch along raw edges before you wash; in fact, you may want to wash your canvas multiple times before attacking your project. Duck canvas has a tighter weave than plain canvas, and as such has a firmer hand. The weave of canvas can be a bit coarse, so it may not be the best idea to line the sleep side of your quilt with it, unless it has been well worn and washed several times.

COTTON

Quilting and fashion-weight cottons are the staple materials featured in my quilts. I've used a combination of my own Parson Gray printed quilting cottons, as well as many shades of the FreeSpirit Designer Essential Solids range. Sewing with these fabrics is quite easy, but keep in mind that cotton tends to shrink, so it's advised to prewash your cottons before sewing. Cotton breathes extremely well, as it is almost pure cellulose, and has a moderate elasticity. No special treatment is needed; just keep pressing as you go. Cotton can stand up to considerable wear under normal conditions, although it's not as tough as linen, canvas, denim, or wool.

DENIM

The familiar fabric of the Americas, denim, is actually cotton twill as defined by its weave (the weft passing under two or more warp threads). Historically, only the warp threads are dyed, which is why your jeans look lighter on the inside, and why, when denim fades, it looks unlike any other fabric. There are many weights of denim; they are measured by the weight of 1 yard [1 m] of fabric in ounces. There are many styles and dyes of the fabric, as well. Depending on these factors, you may need to adjust your sewing needle to accommodate the fabric weight. Well-worn, vintage denim is great for quilting, as it remains very sturdy, yet soft, and can handle rigorous use. The patina of open seams that fray easily can be exploited for great effect, as they are in the Old Glory Quilt (page 69).

LINEN

Linen is a textile that wrinkles easily. It is made from the fibers of the flax plant, but the term *linen* can also refer to the specific weave of a fabric made from cotton, hemp, and other fibers. Linen is cool to the touch and very absorbent. Therefore, it's a great fabric for use in quilts, where you want to retain a lighter feel for hot weather climates or for folks who prefer lighter bedding. Linen can be a bit more expensive than other fabrics, as the process to make linen is more labor-intensive. Linen is a very tough fabric, resistant to abrasion, but the fibers do not stretch; this means that over time they can break down where they are folded or ironed. Linen does shrink and can stand up to high temperatures, but it's still advised to prewash your linen before sewing and press it while still a little damp.

WOOL

It isn't just the fleece of the sheep, and it is neither hair nor fur. *Wool* refers to a fiber from certain types of animals, including sheep, cashmere and mohair from goats, and angora from rabbits. Wool fibers are crimped, which gives the fabric more bulk, and air and water retention. Because of this, wool is a great insulator for and against heat; if you want to make a very warm quilt, make it with wool. Wool fibers are also very elastic, so they can both shrink and stretch, and it can be felted if treated with steam or hot water and agitation. It's best to hand-wash the fabric in cold water and lay flat to dry, reshaping if necessary. You should also use a pressing cloth or roller when pressing. You don't have to worry about fraying or raw seams. It's quite malleable, and it's fairly resistant to wrinkling. Wool is also considered hypoallergenic. The downsides to wool can be its bulky seams; some varieties have a scratchy texture, and you'll need to spot or dry-clean a finished wool quilt. But wool is quite resistant to staining, so that's not too big of an issue.

VINTAGE FABRICS

Common sense is key when shopping for and sewing with vintage textiles. Over time, the fibers wear, become brittle, and are more likely to fail under the strain of sewing. This is fairly easy to tell by simply handling a vintage find. Does it feel dry and coarse to the touch? Rubbing the edges to see how the fabric reacts around the selvage is a simple way to feel if it is a strong or weak fiber. Crimping the fabric in your hand to see how it bounces back helps as well. If the fabric seems reasonable to you, the following tips will help in preparing and cleaning your finds.

○ Chemicals in modern cleaners may react with the dyes in old fabrics. It's usually best to clean old fabrics by old methods. Mild hand washing and soaking in Borax or another mild soap, followed by drying on a line or flattening on a towel, usually work well. Don't wash vintage fabrics in the washing machine, and certainly don't dry them in the dryer, as the heat can further damage the old fibers. It's best to gently squeeze out the remaining water; don't wring.

○ If you have a sturdier cotton that you feel would be fine in the washing machine, it's still best to avoid fabric softeners and softener sheets. They, too, can ruin the fabrics with residue.

○ To press: slowly add temperature as you go, and use a well-padded ironing board. Press from the fabric's **wrong** side while slightly damp. If the fabric seems very delicate, place a white cotton press cloth (like a pillowcase or sheet) on the **wrong** side and press. For wool, a light steaming or hanging of the fabric while dry should remove any wrinkles.

○ If your fabric passes all of these cleaning and drying tests, it should be fine to use going forward. Remember, it's better to find out in advance, rather than after your quilt is completed and gets its first bath!

GRITTY TECHNIQUES FOR GORGEOUS TEXTURE

Part of giving these quilts that worn-out, lived-in feel requires getting a little down and dirty with the materials. Following are some of my go-to methods for distressing and deconstructing fabrics. Each of these techniques will add texture and depth to the different textiles used and bring out each project's own unique character. I call these Gritty Techniques, and have used one or more on several of the quilts in this book. Each project that incorporates these methods will refer you back to this section for guidance and instructions. This can be a messy process, but hey, that's part of the fun! These techniques can lead to some original, gorgeous pieces.

DISTRESSING FABRIC

First, it must be pointed out that distressing fabric is fun, especially for guys who hate to wash clothes. I'm of the ilk who prefer demolition to construction. When it comes to creating that historical and "lived-in" character, to hide blemishes, or just to give the right patina, the only possible mistake with distressing might be getting carried away. There are several techniques and ideas in this section. On the surface, they may seem fairly obvious, but they're really just a jumping-off point for you to discover and experiment with different combinations of abusive, malevolent, and creatively destructive techniques. Go easy at first. You can always add, but you can't take away distressing.

TOOLS FOR DISTRESSING

○ Various grits of sandpaper
○ Pumice stones
○ Wire brushes
○ Scissors or craft knives

DENIM, CANVAS, AND HEAVIER-WEIGHT FABRICS

These fabrics can take quite a bit of abuse, but still, start easy to see how much is needed for the right amount of distressing. Use scraps of fabric to experiment on at first, if you like. Here are several ideas you can use:

O I like to start by laying the fabrics or finished quilts out flat and hitting spots with a lighter grit sandpaper. I work from the larger distressing area, keeping it light, then narrowing in on the area where the most amount of abuse would occur. Generally, for "real" looking distressing, think of the blemishes as a blast site, the most damage in the middle and fading out as it goes away from the center. Use a coarser, heavier grit sandpaper as you work toward the middle of the area, and then if it warrants, you can use a pumice stone or wire brush to work the center.

O If you want it to wear through as a hole, you can cut the hole by bunching up the center and snipping the tip of it off. You'll have to rework the freshly cut hole with the sandpapers and brush to fray the fabric.

O If you want that denim "worn knee" look, you'll need to just really go at it with the sandpaper and pumice to leave the white cross weave intact.

O Another good technique is to use a sharp knife; work back and forth with the side of the blade to shave the fabric.

O Use dirt with a bit of oil to rub the area center out, to stain the threads. This is a pretty aggressive type of distressing, and generally not something I do for the quilts, aside from the boro style (page 33).

Generally, I use the sandpaper and pumice to get the right amount of common wear from dragging and regular use. I then go to work on either fading or staining the fabrics. The sandpapered areas will have a rougher texture that will hold more stain.

LIGHTER QUILTING COTTONS AND LINENS

Basically, you can apply the same methods as above, just back off quite a bit. Depending on the weight of your fabric, it's easy to go too far. Generally, I don't apply much distressing to these weights of fabrics; I only use the techniques for "frayed" edges as needed, and usually this can be created by cutting the size fabrics you need and simply running them through the dryer. I rely instead on other aging techniques (like fading, staining, and dyeing) that are covered next.

STAINING, FADING, AND DYEING FABRIC

Staining and fading techniques are probably the most important steps in creating the vintage character of well-worn fabrics. I list these after distressing only because it's a good idea to do your distressing first; otherwise, the distressed areas may look newer than the rest of the fabric. My favorite techniques are outlined here, including tea and coffee staining, basting and baking, bleach, peroxide, rock salt, and a host of other mad concoctions. With patience, I can definitely say that Mother Nature provides the best, most authentic approach. Dirt, sun, weather, and environment can seal the deal on your quest to speed up time. I try to do all of my staining and fading outside in an area that won't be affected by whatever I'm using, and the sun, combined with a nice breeze, can provide the immediate drying results to see my progress.

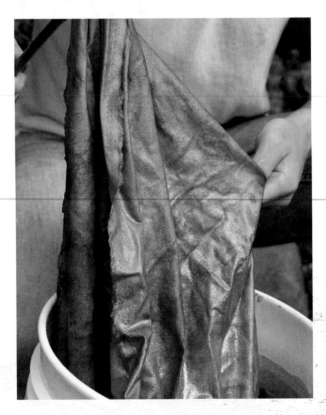

TOOLS AND MATERIALS FOR STAINING, FADING, AND DYEING

- O Coffee (inexpensive, ground variety)
- O Tea (loose and family-size black teas)
- O Large containers (plastic tubs or bins)
- O The sun
- O Bleach (and spray bottle "cleanup" bleaches as well)
- O Pump spray bottles
- O Large sponges
- O Tarp
- O Safety glasses
- O Plenty of long rubber gloves
- O Vinegar
- O Hydrogen peroxide
- O Lemon
- O Epsom or rock salts
- O Fuller's Earth or regular dirt
- O Motor oil
- O Dark stains or paints (oil or acrylic)
- O Indigo dye kit
- O 5-gallon [18-L] bucket
- O RIT or other brand dyes
- O Iron
- O Oven
- O Washing machine and dryer

NOTE: *Wear clothes that you don't mind ruining.*

COFFEE AND TEA STAINING

As the most common, most useful, and also best-smelling of the advanced aging techniques, coffee and tea staining are quite easy. When staining your fabric with either coffee or tea, make sure the fabric is laundered first; do not dry. The fabric should be damp when going into the brew.

COFFEE
Basically, you need a pot or a tub big enough to hold your fabrics, which will be covered with very hot water. I don't like to do this kind of work in the kitchen, so instead of trying to boil a very large pot of water, I make smaller batches of hot water and add them to a large tub or bin in the garage or outdoors. I'm far less pragmatic about the technique and far happier with the results I get by simply putting my fabrics into the bin, covering them with raw dry coffee, letting it fall into the cracks of the fabric, and then adding the water. Where the coffee grounds settle, you'll get darker spots. That gives it a much more authentic look. Obviously, the more coffee you add, and the longer you let it set, the darker your fabrics will get. For a real vintage shade of stain, I keep the fabrics in the hot water for several hours. For another great effect, lay your fabric out on the ground in the sun to dry, and take more grounds and sprinkle them over the wet fabric. You can even spritz them with more water; the grounds will leave small pock prints that simulate natural acid, dirt, and rust aging.

TEA
Use the same technique as coffee, except tea will take longer, and will probably be more expensive in the long run. It also tends to turn your stain a bit brownish-red, as opposed to the nice brown you get with coffee. The number of tea bags you use and how long you let the fabric sit will depend on how dark you want the stain to be. Start with a large pot of boiling water and let your tea steep for at least 15 minutes (longer if you want a stronger brew), then immerse your fabric, keeping as much of it below the water surface for an even absorption. Keep checking your fabric until you get the shade

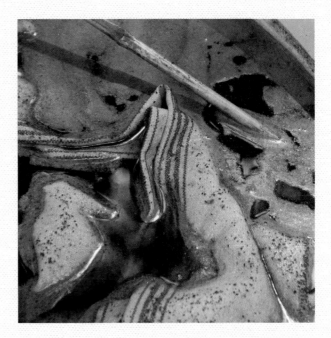

you want. I have let my fabric sit overnight for a deeper stain. Laying tea bags on the drying fabric will give it some interesting dark spots, if you wish. Tea is great if you're looking to create more subtle effects; experiment with using a combination of green tea and lighter black teas to get some nice subtle stained effects.

BAKING FABRIC
Baking fabric is an add-on step to coffee or tea staining, in which you use heat to help set the stain into the fabric, using your oven. Follow the steps for coffee or tea staining as mentioned, and then wring out some, but not too much, of your stain water. Carefully arrange the fabric wadded up on a baking sheet and put it into a 250°F [120°C] oven. Make sure that it's well below the top burners, so it doesn't touch or catch fire. Allow it to bake for around 15 minutes, then remove it, re-wad it into another small pile, and bake again until you start to see the consistency, odd mottling, and coloration you seek. After you're satisfied, you can hang it out to dry, and then press the dry fabric to set the stain (use an older iron if you have one).

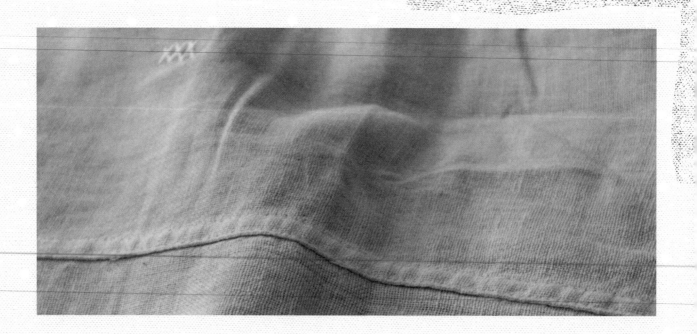

FADING FABRIC

Obviously, the number one way to fade fabric is to leave it out in the sun, for as long as you can. Nothing can achieve a natural look quite like nature! If I want to expedite this process, I use a little bleach. One way is to add some bleach to water (your ratio will depend on how heavy a bleach you want; it's best to start with around 50/50) and put it into a pump spray bottle. I just go over the fabric (hitting some areas a little harder than others) to give it an authentic look. If you're doing this outside, watch out for the breeze! You can quickly ruin your clothes, kill plants, or bleach out whatever you're working on or around. Be sure to use some kind of a tarp, and always wear rubber gloves. A more direct route is to add more water to your 50/50 bleach and water solution and, using a sponge (wring it out well), dab the mixture onto areas of the fabric and rub the sponge into the areas you want to fade more. You can then rinse the treated fabric in the washing machine, by itself, in a cold water cycle. Other great fading agents that are less toxic are vinegar, hydrogen peroxide, or lemon juice. All of these work really well. You can follow the same formulas given for bleach, or experiment with different strengths. Also, Epsom or rock salts in a bath can give lighter fabrics a bit of a blotchy appearance as they fade the color.

A note on fading black fabric: Bleach will probably yield an odd reddish or even yellow tint to most black fabrics. You may want to try other methods. It's harder than it seems to get that nice gray fade, and the more natural methods, especially sun fading, usually work better. The best thing to do is to try a sample first, using different techniques. Denim, navy, reds, and greens tend to fade more easily than black dyed cottons.

NATURAL STAINING

If you want to get a really authentic dirty look, bury it! If you have a wooded area, the best thing is to just leave it under some leaves for a week or so and throw a little bit of dirt on it, or use Fuller's Earth if you have to do it inside (but that won't quite give you the same effect). It seems counterintuitive to anything you might want to do, but you'll get amazing effects, especially if it rains, since you need a little moisture to really get the best look. This can be a great thing to do after you've coffee or tea stained if you feel the patina just isn't harsh enough. I will, on occasion, even spatter my fabrics with motor oil or dark brown deck stain (using a small brush) to replicate mildew stains or acidic burns.

FABRIC DYEING AND PAINT STAINING

I've been dyeing, or at least attempting to dye fabrics since I was a teenager. It's a great way to get specific colors and textures to suit your particular project.

INDIGO

Indigo dyeing is easy, fun, and smelly, although it has come a long way since the days of adjusting the pH by urinating in the vats (the same can be said for woad dyeing). And I can't stress this enough: Do this one outside. I recommend that you buy an all-in-one kit for indigo dyeing. These kits are available through Dharma Trading Company and contain very easy instructions and all of the ingredients you need. In fact, Dharma Trading Company has everything you need for dyeing, including great instructions for all of the products they sell. That said, I'm approaching the dyeing process like all of the other processes, to give patina and "mess up" the evenness of the dye bath. When dyeing my indigo, I actually throw a little dirt into the mixture and use a dirty 5-gallon [18-L] bucket. I crumple the fabric into the mixture and let it set for around 40 minutes. Upon removing it from the dye bath, I let it oxidize in the sun by placing it in a pile of leaves or gravel. It comes out yellow, then bright green (see photo on page 16), and as the oxygen reacts with the dye very quickly, it turns blue. It's messy, and you'll need to wear rubber gloves unless you want blue hands. Spritzing certain areas with bleach after the bath will create pre-faded areas. Also, this is a good time to add any other color patina like oil stains or paint. You can let the fabric dry and re-soak it in the bath if you want it to be a darker blue, rinse it out with a hose, or run it through your washing machine and dryer (by itself, obviously). Wash out your machine with a bit of bleach and a rinse cycle afterward.

ROUGH DYEING

What I refer to as "rough dyeing" simply means adding aggregates (like RIT or other brand dyes) to your dye bath—things that will add a mottle or texture to the way the dye takes to your fabric. Simply follow the instructions on the dyes that you buy, but then add in a bit of cooking oil to make pockets of resist, blended with some other darker powder dye and dirt or gravel. For an interesting vintage effect, "fold" the aggregates and oil into the fabric, layering and folding, then wad it up and hold it together with rubber bands in different configurations. It makes the dye take hold in the spaces between and can give a very nice, subtle patina to the color. Doing this in layers, unfolding, and then resetting the aggregates and putting it back into the dye bath can give a great mottled effect. You may even want to hit it with a little bit of bleach from a spray bottle in certain areas as soon as it comes out of the bath, before you rinse or dry the fabric.

QUILT-MAKING STEPS

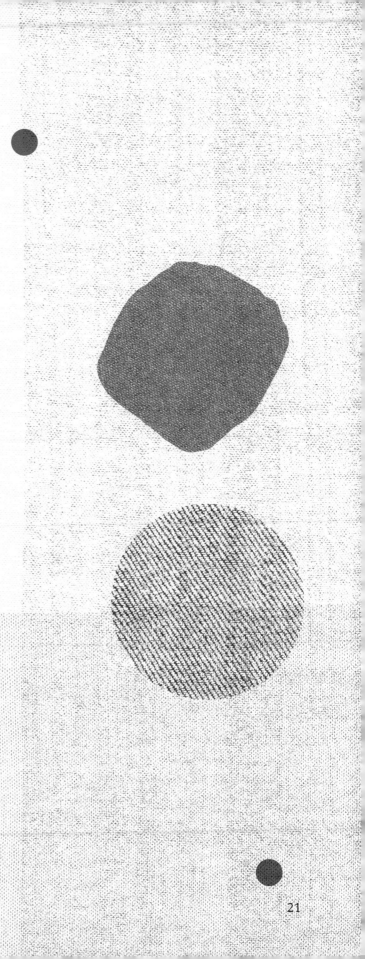

All of the projects in this book have steps that are used to complete the quilt once the Quilt Top has been pieced or sewn together. Each project will list references to the different techniques that are used for assembling the quilt, joining the layers, and then finishing the quilt. The detailed instructions for each of these steps and techniques follow.

PREP FOR QUILTING

A quilt is most often made of three layers: the Quilt Top, the batting, and the Quilt Back. These layers are also known as the Quilt Sandwich.

QUILT TOP

The Quilt Top is the decorative top layer of a quilt. It is made from pieces of fabric sewn together into a design. Although not included in this book, a Quilt Top can also consist of one piece of fabric allowing for the quilting stitches to dominate and create a design. The Quilt Back (also known as backing) typically consists of fabric yardage that covers the batting at the back of a Quilt Sandwich.

BATTING

The middle layer or batting in a quilt is what will add loft while also adding warmth to the finished project. There are many different types of batting and each has its own purpose and advantages.

For most of the quilts in this book, we chose to use cotton flannel for the batting. Flannel makes the quilt feel more like a blanket and doesn't add loft to the quilt, as traditional batting would. Prewash the flannel before construction, as the cotton fabric does shrink quite a bit. Like the backing fabric, flannel isn't wide enough to cover the entire width of the quilts, so you will need to piece it in the same way as you piece the backing fabric.

For the Forged Block Quilt (page 51) and Carpetbagger Quilt (page 153), we chose to use a low-loft, cotton batting to give the quilts added weight and warmth. Cotton batting is also a good choice when using an all-over quilting design whether hand or machine quilting.

QUILT BACK

Many of the quilts in this book measure 72" [183 cm] square. Since fabric yardage typically measures 42" to 44" [107 to 112 cm] wide, we instruct you, in each pattern, to piece the backing lengthwise in order to completely cover the back of the quilt. If you choose to do so, consider making a more creative backing by adding a design detail from the Quilt Top or create more intricate piecing for your Quilt Back. We chose to simplify the backing so there is more focus on the Quilt Top.

LAYERING A QUILT SANDWICH

Once your quilt layers are ready, layer them into a Quilt Sandwich by following these steps (if you are spray basting, go directly to the instructions on page 23):

1. On a flat, open space, such as a large table or floor, lay out your prepared backing fabric (Quilt Back), **wrong** side up. Smooth flat to remove any wrinkles.
2. Center and lay your batting on top of the Quilt Back; smooth out any wrinkles.
3. Center the Quilt Top on the batting with the **right** side up; smooth out any wrinkles.
4. Once the layers are laid out entirely flat and without wrinkles, baste all the layers together to temporarily hold them in place before quilting. Use safety pins or a needle and thread as follows.

BASTING METHODS

Either Saftey Pin Basting or Thread Basting are preferred methods to use when planning to tie or embroider your quilt layers together—a much more organic way of quilting. Spray Basting is ideal for Machine Quilting using either Stitch-in-the-Ditch, Straight-Line, or Shadow methods of quilting. Spray Basting gives the Quilt Sandwich much more stability, as the layers become fixed and will not shift. This helps make your job easier, avoiding puckering in the top and/or bottom fabric of your quilt as the Quilt Sandwich travels under the presser foot.

SAFETY PIN BASTING

Starting from the center of the quilt and working toward the outside edges, use the safety pins to form a grid, with the rows and columns about 6" [15 cm] apart, unless otherwise specified in the project instructions.

THREAD BASTING

Thread basting can be used for any type of quilt; however, it is best known to be used for quilts you'll be quilting by hand, such as the Coal Mine Quilt (page 119).

1. Using contrasting thread and a large needle, work from the center of the Quilt Sandwich up toward the top edge, through all three layers, and hand sew one row of long running stitches (page 33). Return to the center and sew one row using the same size stitches at a 90-degree angle to the right-hand edge of your quilt.

2. Continue by stitching from the center to the bottom edge, and then from the center to the left-hand edge to complete a large (+). Continue basting by spacing long running stitch rows about 4" [10 cm] apart. Always start at the center horizontal and center vertical row that you stitched first and stitch out to the edges.

3. When finished, you'll have a 4" [10 cm] square grid of running stitches.

SPRAY BASTING

1. Lay the Quilt Back **wrong** side up on a flat surface, such as a floor (preferably) or a large table. If using a floor, use masking tape or painter's tape to tape the fabric taut.

2. Next, lay the batting on top of the backing, **right** side up and smooth flat. Gently fold back the top edge of the batting to meet the bottom edge. At the fold of the batting, spray an even coat of batting spray about 6" [15 cm] wide horizontally across the width of the batting. Fold the sprayed portion of the batting back onto the backing fabric and smooth in place. Continue spraying in 6" [15 cm] wide, even coats horizontally, smoothing as you go, until you've finished with the top half of the batting.

3. Repeat these steps with the bottom half of the batting. When finished, lay the Quilt Top, **right** side up, on top of the batting and smooth flat.

4. As you did to adhere your batting to your backing fabric, you'll do the same to adhere your batting to your Quilt Top, by pulling the top edge of the Quilt Top even with its bottom edge. At the fold of the Quilt Top, spray a 6" [15 cm] wide, even coat of batting spray horizontally across the width of the batting. Place a 6" [15 cm] wide section of the Quilt Top on top of the sprayed portion of the batting and smooth in place.

5. Continue this same process until you've finished with the top half of the batting, then repeat these steps for the bottom half to finish spray basting the Quilt Sandwich.

You're now ready to begin quilting or tying your layers together.

QUILTING METHODS

Quilting is the process of sewing the three layers (the Quilt Top, the batting, and the Quilt Back) together to make a quilt. The projects contained in this book offer a variety of ways to achieve a finished look that works well with each of the designs. Some of the quilts are sewn together using hand-stitching methods and some by machine. There are several projects that use a combination of hand stitching and machine quilting.

HAND STITCHING

When hand stitching the quilting stitches in this book, we used embroidery thread that comes on a spool. This type of embroidery thread can be used with your sewing machine, too. The type of embroidery thread (either cotton or wool) and the colors we used are included within each pattern. Use an embroidery needle when Tying and hand stitching embroidery, and while creating the small boro running stitches for the Coal Mine Quilt (page 119).

Tying the Quilt

A simple, knotted tying method was chosen for the Navajo Blanket Quilt (page 37), Grainery Quilt (page 41), and 1890s Trader's Quilt (page 83). We also created a new form of tying a quilt just for this book using a cross-stitch in the form of X's, used on the Maritime Quilt (page 55) and Arrow Quilt (page 159) (Triple-X), and the Skelton Crew Quilt (page 103) (Double-X).

In the Basting Methods section, you will Safety Pin Baste through all three layers of the Quilt Sandwich in a predetermined grid. In the grid you create, safety pins mark the points where you will tie the quilt.

Thread your embroidery needle with the recommended embroidery thread. Do not make a knot at the end of the length of thread.

Beginning in the center of the Quilt Sandwich, remove a safety pin. In the same spot, insert your threaded embroidery needle down through the Quilt Sandwich. Pull your thread through to the back, leaving a 3" [7.5 cm] tail of thread on the Quilt Top. From the Quilt Back side of the Quilt Sandwich, insert your needle up through the layers, approximately ½" [12 mm] away from the original insertion, and gently pull the thread through, keeping the starting 3" [7.5 cm] tail on top. Once again, insert your needle into your first stitch hole to the Quilt Back, and up through the second stitch hole, returning the needle to the Quilt Top. Snip the long thread to a 3" [7.5 cm] tail and tie off the two tails with a double knot. Finally, trim the tails to the size suggested in the pattern. Continue with this same process at each safety pin that you used on the Quilt Top until all pins have been replaced with ties.

Double-X or Triple-X Hand Stitches

This quilting technique is similar to Tying where two or three "X's" are hand stitched side-by-side, in measured places on the Quilt Top. You can see the Triple-X stitch on the Maritime Quilt (page 55) and the Arrow Quilt (page 159), and the Double-X stitch on the Skeleton Crew Quilt (page 103). Follow the specific instructions for the project and thread an embroidery needle with either cotton or wool embroidery thread; do not tie a knot at the end. Beginning at the back of the Quilt Sandwich, pull the length of thread up through the layers, leaving a 3" [7.5 cm] tail at the back. Using long, narrow diagonal stitches, whip stitch twice (or three times) in one direction where you want the "X's" to go, then whip stitch in the opposite direction, creating the Double/Triple-X Stitch. Tie the beginning and ending tails into a double knot on the back and trim the tails to 1" [2.5 cm] to finish.

MACHINE QUILTING

Machine Quilting techniques are used on the English Cross Quilt (page 133) and Southwest Passage Quilt (page 141) (Shadow Stitching); Grainery Quilt (page 41) and Old Glory Quilt (page 69) (Double Topstitch Seam); Bear Paw Quilt (page 89), World's Fair Quilt (page 95), Painted Desert Quilt (page 109), Bull's-Eye Quilt (page 147) and Carpetbagger Quilt (page 153) (Stitch-in-the-Ditch); and the Iron Bars Quilt (page 47), Forged Block Quilt (page 51), Horse Blanket Quilt (page 63), Fort Battery Quilt (page 75) and Falling Wind Quilt (page 125) (Straight Line Quilting).

When quilting with a machine, be sure to test your stitch length before you begin, because every sewing machine is unique. Use a walking foot when stitching straight lines or slight curves on a quilt, and wear quilting gloves or rubber fingers to assist in guiding your quilt as you sew.

Because the quilts in this book are considered more utilitarian, we recommend that you use a longer machine quilting stitch length (3.5 to 4) than you would normally use for piecing. We suggest making a stitch-length swatch: take two 6" [15 cm] squares of a solid fabric and a 6" [15 cm] square of cotton batting or flannel placed between them to make a mini Quilt Sandwich. Using a straight stitch and contrasting thread, machine stitch a few rows through the layers using several different stitch lengths. Jot down the length size with a marking pen or pencil next to each row of stitches. Keep adjusting your stitch length until you like what you see. When finished, consider keeping your quilted stitch-length swatch nearby as a reference for future projects.

Before you begin quilting, roll up the quilt tightly with quilt clips to keep the bulk in the throat of your sewing machine from interfering with your sewing.

TIP: *Pre-wind several bobbins before beginning to quilt, as Machine Quilting uses a lot of thread.*

Shadow Stitching

The Shadow Stitching method of quilting is quite easy to achieve. It is simply stitching around the outline of a shape on either the inside or the outside of the shape's edge; it is also known as Outline Quilting or Echo Quilting. Shadow Stitching is used on the English Cross Quilt (page 133) and on the Southwest Passage Quilt (page 141). Each of these projects has specific details on Shadow Stitching in its instructions.

Double Topstitch Seam

The Double Topstitch Seam resembles the double topstitching found on denim jeans. Machine stitch the seams of your quilt ⅛" [3 mm] away from the seam with a slightly longer stitch length than normal. When finished with the stitching, move the quilt slightly and sew a second row of stitching ¼" to ⅜" [6 mm to 1 cm] away from the first row. Backstitch at the beginning and end of each row.

On some of the quilts that use this technique, like the Grainery Quilt (page 41) and Old Glory Quilt (page 69), Double Topstitch to within 2" to 3" [5 to 7.5 cm] from the edge of the Quilt Top, and use a Quilt Finishing Technique before completing the quilting.

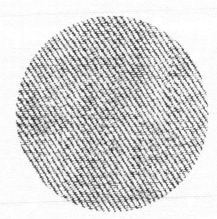

Stitch-in-the-Ditch

This quilting technique is the easiest to do and great for beginners. It is used on the Bear Paw Quilt (page 89), World's Fair Quilt (page 95), Painted Desert Quilt (page 109), and Carpetbagger Quilt (page 153). We give you instructions on what elements to Stitch-in-the-Ditch within each of these projects. However, here are some basic guidelines on how to sew this method of quilting:

1. Plan your sewing before you begin. Ask yourself what you'll be quilting first.
2. Starting in the center of the quilt, line up your presser foot to straddle a seam and insert your needle in "the ditch" (where the seams meet). Anchor your first stitch, and then continue sewing in-the-ditch according to the pattern's instructions.
3. When you come to the end of a "ditch," anchor your last stitch, then move your quilt to the next spot, always working from the center out.

There are several quilts that combine two different techniques of quilting: Fort Battery Quilt (page 75) (Stitch-in-the-Ditch and Diagonal Straight Line Quilting), English Cross Quilt (page 133) (Stitch-in-the-Ditch and Shadow Stitching), and Arrow Quilt (page 159) (Straight Line Quilting and Triple-X Hand Stitch).

Straight Line Quilting

This quilting technique is also great for beginners. Use a ruler and fabric marking pen or pencil to mark the quilting grid called out in the pattern. Beginning in the center of the Quilt Top along a marked line, anchor your first stitch, then sew a straight line of stitches to within a few inches [5 to 7.5 cm] of the edge of the quilt. Return to your starting point, then repeat this process of sewing in the opposite direction. Continue sewing as instructed in the pattern.

Diagonal Straight Line Quilting

This is the same technique as Straight Line Quilting, but the rows of stitching are machine stitched diagonally on the Quilt Top. Overlap the diagonal stitches on the quilt to create a lattice effect, such as on the Iron Bars Quilt (page 47).

FINISHING THE QUILT EDGES

There are several different ways to finish off the raw edges of your quilt. This book contains instructions on how to make traditional Double Fold (French Fold) Binding, a Fold Finish Edge, and Self-Binding.

DOUBLE FOLD BINDING

1. Using the binding strips you cut in the project instructions, place two strips perpendicular to each other with the **right** sides together, overlapping by ¼" [6 mm]. With a pencil or marking pen, draw a diagonal line on the **wrong** side of the fabric, then pin and stitch along the diagonal line. (See Diagram 1.)
2. Trim the seam allowance to ¼" [6 mm] and press open. (See Diagram 2.) Repeat until you have created a strip the length required for the project.
3. With the **wrong** sides together, line up the long, raw edges and press a crease along the entire folded edge, lengthwise.
4. To attach the binding, place the Quilt Top in front of you, **right** side facing up. Start at the center of the bottom edge and match the raw edges of the binding and the quilt, pinning as you go, and stopping at the first corner.
5. Leaving the first 5" [12 cm] of the binding unstitched, begin sewing using a ¼" [6 mm] seam allowance. Stop ¼" [6 mm] from the first corner; backstitch. Remove the quilt from your machine and clip the threads.
6. To form a neat, mitered corner, fold the binding away from the corner, forming a 45-degree angle. (See Diagram 3.)
7. Next, fold the binding down, even with the next side's raw edge, and pin it in place. Leave the folded edge of the binding even with the first edge that was sewn. (See Diagram 4.) Begin stitching again at the corner's edge of the quilt, backstitching as you start. Continue to pin and sew along the edge, stopping ¼" [6 mm] from the next corner, and backstitch again.
8. Repeat Steps 6 and 7 to miter the remaining corners, sewing the rest of the binding in place. Stopping 10" [25 cm] from where you first began, backstitch.
9. Cut the binding so it overlaps the beginning edge by 6" [15 cm]. Fold the beginning edge ½" [12 mm] under (toward the **wrong** side of the binding) and press.

10. Insert the end of the binding under the beginning folded edge. Pin and stitch the rest of the binding in place to finish.

11. Press the binding away from the Quilt Top.

12. Turn your quilt over so that the Quilt Back is facing up. Fold the binding over the raw edge from the front of the quilt to the back and line up the folded edge of the binding so it just covers the ¼" [6 mm] stitching that attached it to the Quilt Top. Adjust the mitered corners and pin them in place; slipstitch (see page 165) the binding in place around all four sides, including corners, to finish.

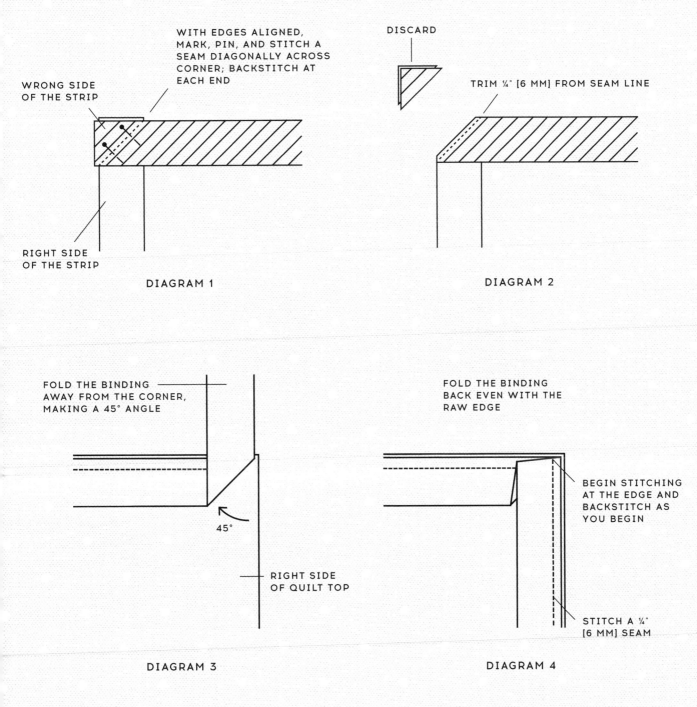

WITH EDGES ALIGNED, MARK, PIN, AND STITCH A SEAM DIAGONALLY ACROSS CORNER; BACKSTITCH AT EACH END

WRONG SIDE OF THE STRIP

RIGHT SIDE OF THE STRIP

DIAGRAM 1

DISCARD

TRIM ¼" [6 MM] FROM SEAM LINE

DIAGRAM 2

FOLD THE BINDING AWAY FROM THE CORNER, MAKING A 45° ANGLE

45°

RIGHT SIDE OF QUILT TOP

DIAGRAM 3

FOLD THE BINDING BACK EVEN WITH THE RAW EDGE

BEGIN STITCHING AT THE EDGE AND BACKSTITCH AS YOU BEGIN

STITCH A ¼" [6 MM] SEAM

DIAGRAM 4

FOLD FINISH EDGE

1. Beginning along one side of the Quilt Sandwich, use your 6" x 24" [15 x 61 cm] ruler, rotary cutter, and cutting mat to trim the Quilt Back and batting even with the Quilt Top.

2. Lay the Quilt Sandwich back on your cutting mat, then pull the Quilt Top and Quilt Back away to expose the batting. Using your ruler and rotary cutter and being careful not to cut into the Quilt Top or Quilt Back, trim ½" [12 mm] from the batting around all four sides. (See Diagram 1.)

3. Place the Quilt Sandwich on a large table or workspace with the Quilt Top facing up. At the first corner, fold the corner of the Quilt Back at a 45-degree angle over the corner of the batting, as shown, then fold the top edge of the Quilt Back over ½" [12 mm] onto the batting; pin in place. (See Diagram 2.)

4. As you did in Step 3 and along the left side of the corner you're working on, fold the Quilt Back over ½" [12 mm] onto the batting and pin in place to make your first mitered corner. (See Diagram 3.)

5. Continue to fold and pin the Quilt Back onto the batting along each side and miter each corner, as instructed.

6. Using these same techniques (Steps 3 to 5), miter the Quilt Top corners and pin the sides under ½" [12 mm] to meet the folded edge of the Quilt Back; pin through all three layers to secure the folded edges together to prepare for sewing. (See Diagram 4.)

7. The pattern instructions will explain the type of stitching we recommend to stitch the edges of your quilt together, then refer to one of the three following methods.

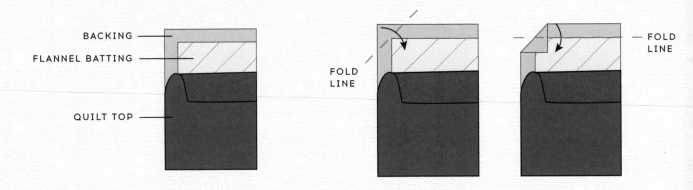

BACKING

FLANNEL BATTING

QUILT TOP

FOLD LINE

FOLD LINE

DIAGRAM 1

DIAGRAM 2

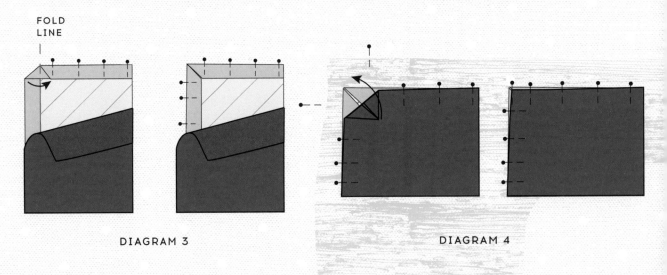

FOLD LINE

DIAGRAM 3

DIAGRAM 4

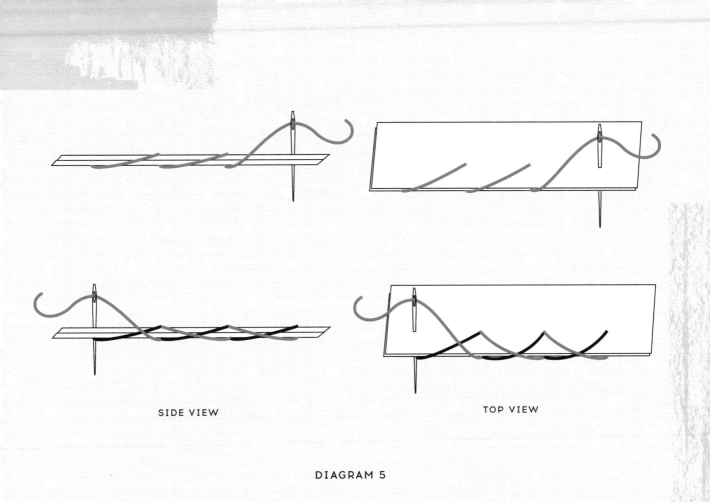

SIDE VIEW   TOP VIEW

DIAGRAM 5

a. **Single Stitch Edge (Machine):** In the center of one side of the Quilt Top, place the machine needle down ⅛" [3 mm] from the folded edges of the Quilt Sandwich and backstitch (see Glossary, page 164). Continue to sew along the outside edge of your quilt, backstitching and pivoting at each corner. End your stitching where you started and backstitch to finish.

b. **Double Stitch Edge (Machine):** When finished, this stitched edge will resemble the double top-stitching found on denim jeans. Referring to Single Stitch Edge instructions, machine stitch around all four sides of your quilt. When finished with the first round of stitching, shift the edge of the quilt slightly and needle-down ¼" to ⅜" [6 mm to 1 cm] inside of the first round of stitching. In the same manner, stitch around all four sides of the quilt. The Arrow Quilt (page 159) uses the Double Stitch Edge for finishing.

c. **X-Edge Stitch (Hand):** Three quilts in this book, Maritime Quilt (page 55), Horse Blanket Quilt (page 63), and Skeleton Crew Quilt (page 103), use the hand-stitched edge we created called the X-Edge Stitch. First, prepare a Fold Finish Edge (see page 28). Follow Diagram 5 and simply whip stitch in one direction around the entire outside edge of the Quilt Top; then whip stitch in the opposite direction, creating an "X" across the first row of whip stitches to finish.

TIP: *Consider using monofilament thread and follow the instructions for the Single Stitch Edge with your sewing machine around the outside edge of the Quilt Sandwich before applying the X-Edge Stitch to the outside edge of the quilt.*

SELF-BINDING

This binding uses a Quilt Backing that is trimmed larger than the Quilt Top and batting. Our more primitive method is made without mitered corners. We developed this method to fit in with the style of our quilts. This method of Self-Binding is used on the Iron Bars Quilt (page 47) and Carpetbagger Quilt (page 153).

Referring to the project instructions, trim the batting even with the Quilt Top, then trim the sides of the backing to the measurements stated in the project. Beginning in the middle of the right-hand edge of the Quilt Sandwich, fold over one-half of the exposed backing fabric once along the entire length and finger press (see Diagram 1). Fold over the entire right-hand length a second time, covering ¼" [6 mm] of the Quilt Top edge; pin and sew in place (see Diagram 2). Do the same on the left-hand side of the Quilt Top. Continue by using the same folding, pinning, and sewing technique along the top and bottom edges (see Diagrams 3 and 4) to finish your Quilt Top.

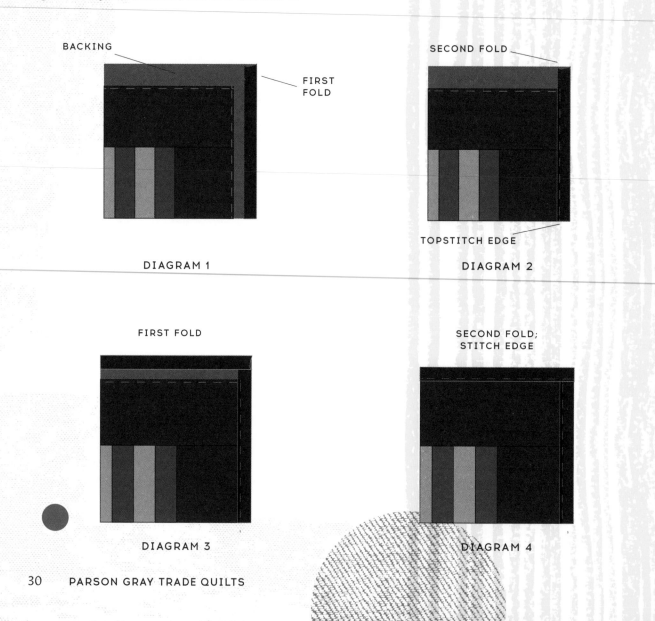

BACKING

FIRST FOLD

DIAGRAM 1

SECOND FOLD

TOPSTITCH EDGE

DIAGRAM 2

FIRST FOLD

DIAGRAM 3

SECOND FOLD; STITCH EDGE

DIAGRAM 4

APPLIQUÉ STITCHING

Appliqué is a technique whereby a single layer of fabric is cut into a shape and stitched to a base layer. The outline of the shape can either be hand stitched or machine stitched, and the edge of the shape can be either left raw or turned under, depending on how rough or finished you want the end result to be. Here are the appliqué methods we used in the book.

FREEZER PAPER APPLIQUÉ

With **wrong** side up, trace the paper appliqué template from the template sheet (templates in the book include seam allowance) onto the **wrong** side of the fabric. Cut the shape from the fabric and set aside. NOTE: *We have you trace the template onto poster board when the appliqué shape is oversized for ease of tracing.*

Trim the seam allowance from the paper appliqué template and, with **right** side up, trace onto the matte, paper side of the freezer paper; cut out the appliqué shape.

With the waxy side facing up, center and pin the matte, paper side of the template to the **wrong** side of your fabric shape. Using the tip of your iron, fold the fabric seam allowance onto the waxy side of the appliqué template and press in place around the entire edge of the template. Carefully trim the seam allowance minimally in places where there is excessive fabric to reduce bulk (at corners and points). Also, trim the seam allowance in a perpendicular manner in tight areas, such as where a right angle would occur, or around arcs; trim to within a few threads of the template's edge. Tuck frayed edges at the back so that they will not be seen on the **right** side of the appliqué.

Position and pin the prepared appliqué shape onto the base fabric and hand sew in place, or machine sew using a straight stitch around the outside perimeter.

At the back of the base fabric, snip an opening in the center of the appliquéd shape and trim to within ¼" [6 mm] of the hand or machine stitches to reduce bulk and to remove the freezer paper.

MACHINE APPLIQUÉ

Position and pin the prepared (finished or raw edge) appliqué shape onto the base fabric and machine stitch in place using a straight stitch. At the back of the base fabric, snip an opening in the center of the appliquéd shape and trim to within ¼" [6 mm] of the machine-stitched outline to reduce bulk. Straight-stitch Machine Appliqué was used on the Arrow Quilt (page 159).

RAW EDGE APPLIQUÉ

An unfinished edge to an appliqué shape that is machine stitched to the base fabric is what defines Raw Edge Appliqué. Use paper-backed fusible web to help stabilize the appliqué shape as follows.

Place the **wrong** side of the appliqué template up and position it on the paper side of the paper-backed fusible web; trace the shape with a pencil and cut out the shape. Place the trimmed shape onto the **wrong** side of the suggested appliqué fabric and iron in place according to the manufacturer's instructions; cut the paper appliqué shape from the cloth.

Remove the paper from the back of the fabric appliqué shape and position it on the **right** side of the base fabric; iron it in place. Allow the shape to cool. Using a straight stitch, sew ¼" [6 mm] inside the raw edge of the shape to appliqué it to the base fabric.

The Grainery Quilt (page 41), Forged Block Quilt (page 51), 1890s Trader's Quilt (page 83), Bear Paw Quilt (page 89), World's Fair Quilt (page 95), and Skeleton Crew Quilt (page 103) use Raw Edge Appliqué. Not all use paper-backed fusible web. See individual patterns for instructions.

EMBROIDERY STITCHES

We love how the hand embroidery stitches we chose to use in this book bring visual and textural interest to the quilt designs. The stitches can be seen throughout the book in a variety of uses: to enhance a bound edge, tie a quilt together, or even outline an appliqué shape.

BLANKET STITCH

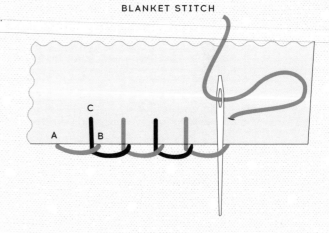

BACK STITCH

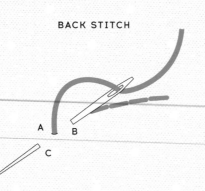

BACK STITCH

The Back Stitch is a straight stitch and is worked from right to left.

Thread your embroidery needle and make a knot at the end of the long thread. Begin making your first stitch by bringing your needle up from the bottom side of your fabric and pull the thread through (A). Placing the needle's point ⅛" [3 mm] behind your first stitch, begin sending your needle to the back of your fabric (B), but before you send the needle all the way through, bring the point of your needle up about ⅛" [3 mm] in front of your first stitch (C); pull your needle through to complete your first Back Stitch. Continue Back Stitching until you've completed your row of stitching and tie off at the back of your project.

MODIFIED BLANKET STITCH

The Blanket Stitch works from left to right and is typically used to finish off the edge of a blanket. This stitch was used for added interest on the corners of some of the small patches placed on the Coal Mine Quilt (page 119) before making the Boro Stitches (page 33).

Thread your embroidery needle with two strands of cotton embroidery thread and knot the long ends together. From the back of the quilt, poke the needle up a few inches (5 to 7.5 mm) to the left of the corner of the patch you're working on (point A). Approximately ¼" [6 mm] to the right of point A, drop your needle down through the layers (point B) and bring the tip of your needle up vertically, approximately ¼" [6 mm] into the patch through the layers to the Quilt Top at point C. Before pulling the long, working thread all the way through, dip the needle down under the loop created between points A and B, and pull the long thread all the way through to make your first stitch. Continue making stitches in this manner and tie off at the back when finished.

BORO STITCH OR RUNNING STITCH

The Boro Stitch is used on the Coal Mine Quilt (page 119). All of the stitches on the quilt were made using a few different colors of ivory embroidery thread.

Thread your embroidery needle with one long strand of cotton embroidery thread and knot the end. Starting a few inches [5 to 7.5 mm] away from your fabric patch at the back side of your quilt, pull your needle and thread through the fabric. Begin loading stitches onto your needle by pushing the needle through the fabric, taking several tight up-and-down stitches in a straight line, and then pulling the needle through; do this through all three layers of your Quilt Sandwich. Continue this sewing technique, loading stitches onto your needle and pulling it through the fabric, until your row is complete; start a new row about ¼" [6 mm] away from the first row. Cover each patch entirely. We chose to sometimes tie off threads at the top side of the quilt to add interest; tie off ends by using the end of the old working thread with the end of the new thread. Do the same if you wish. Refer to images of the Coal Mine Quilt (page 119) for reference.

CROSS STITCH

Our Cross Stitch is different from most Cross Stitches you'll meet. Ours are taller than they are wide, and we created them especially for our Double-X or Triple-X hand-stitching method of Tying a quilt. The stitch begins at the lower left corner of the finished series of X's you'll be making. In some cases, you'll be Cross Stitching a Double-X, and with other quilts you'll be stitching a Triple-X. We'll tell you what to use in each pattern. All X's do not have to be exact unless you want them to be. In other words, it's okay if some of the X's in a series are thinner or not as tall as their mates. We sewed our X's from left to right and then from right to left to complete the sets of X's. See Double-X or Triple-X Hand Stitches (page 24).

If you are doing the Cross Stitch as an X-Edge Stitch (page 29), it's easiest to do all your whip stitches in one direction around the entire Quilt Top edge, and then reverse the whip stitch in the opposite direction to finish.

THE QUILTS

I call my book *Trade Quilts* because these striking ragtags are influenced by antique designs that would have been of high value in low places, like pelts, woven rugs, or of course, wool trade blankets. Built for survival, and showing the wear to prove it, they would have been thrown over the counter in a Yukon outpost, laid out on the Arizona desert floor, hung to dry above the snow outside of a yurt, used to cover up a wounded Union soldier, or thrown under the saddle of a horse. In my global travels, I've been lucky to absorb a rich vocabulary of tribal and cultural influences: Japanese boro, Navajo weaving, Egyptian tent making, German folk art, and so on. It affects all that I do. There are a few "traditional" designs thrown in, such as the Drunkard's Path design in my Carpetbagger Quilt (page 153), and a folksy, loose interpretation of a Bear Paw Quilt (page 89). Yes, it's pretty obvious that these are intended to be guy-friendly designs—something to hang in the entry of the man-cave, perhaps. There's a conspicuous absence of flowers.

I developed and designed these quilts to run a range of expression, ease, and technique. They also incorporate an array of materials, from thrift store denim and old shirts to canvas sacks and off-the-rack quilting cottons. As someone who designs fabrics, I'd love it if you used my prints in your projects, but I was also excited about how little money I had to spend repurposing old jeans, wool skirts, flannel shirts, and old sacks to make these designs work, and work well. I didn't even raid my own closet. I spent a very small amount of money on vintage denim and wool to make the Coal Mine Quilt (page 119). Pretty cool.

The less-than-distressing part of this book is that distressing, or roughing things up a bit, may be the most unique part. Don rubber gloves and stain, fade, bake, perhaps even bleach your way to creative nirvana. Most of the ideas in that section (pages 13 to 19) are the same ones used by Hollywood costume designers and fashion brands that focus on the worn and torn. Applying texture and wear is a way to take away the preciousness of a quilt. It's not meant as historical trickery; rather, it's a way to immediately introduce the quilt into your nesting world, not as an art piece for the back of the couch, or on the wall, but as intended: a practical and beautiful way to keep warm. Nobody worries about grabbing that worn old quilt; it has seen tougher times. The humility of patina is a subtle observation that allows us to embrace imperfection. It is something that I've applied to my graphic art for so many years; it's thrilling to do it with quilts.

Each quilt outlined in this book will be given a "How Tough?" rating from one to five, with one being the easier quilts to accomplish and five, being the toughest. Compared to most other quilts, even my fives are not that difficult for an experienced sewer, but they will take more time than the others in this book. I also present a bulleted list of the techniques used for each quilt, so you can see whether there are specific distressing, staining, or other techniques used on the quilt in the picture. That doesn't mean you need to use them! It's just a reference. You may want a perfectly clean version of the quilt at hand.

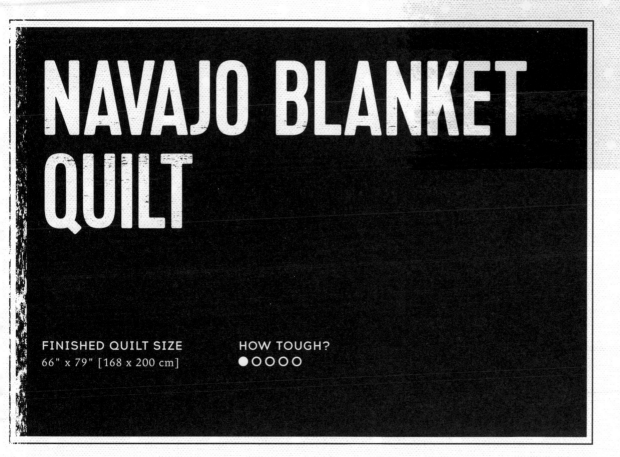

NAVAJO BLANKET QUILT

FINISHED QUILT SIZE
66" x 79" [168 x 200 cm]

HOW TOUGH?
●○○○○

Another one of those fantastic finds that I seem to see everywhere, this quilt is made using a nice soft reproduction Navajo blanket. I picked it up at a vintage shop for next to nothing. The vintage yardage running down the sides is a great old heavy-cotton duck stripe, all vintage. It may be hard to exactly replicate this quilt, but the idea is for you to find your own style of pieces like this, and the pattern here gives you simple instructions to assemble from your stash. The "tough" part is the fun part: finding the right materials. The rest is easy!

FABRICS AND SUPPLIES

- Vintage blanket for the quilt center *(We used a reproduction Navajo blanket, measuring 50" x 80" [127 x 203 cm].)*
- Vintage duck cloth, denim, or other heavyweight fabric for side borders *(Should measure at least 20" [50 cm] wide and as long as the blanket.)*
- Coordinating backing fabric that measures 10" [25 cm] wider and 10" [25 cm] longer than the finished Quilt Top *(You may need to piece a few lengths together to cover the width of the Quilt Top. We used 5 yards [4.6 m].)*
- Ivory flannel fabric for batting that measures 10" [25 cm] wider and 10" [25 cm] longer than the finished Quilt Top *(You may need to piece a few lengths together to cover the width of the Quilt Top. We used 5 yards [4.6 m].)*
- Coordinating cotton thread for piecing.
- One large spool of ivory cotton embroidery thread for quilting

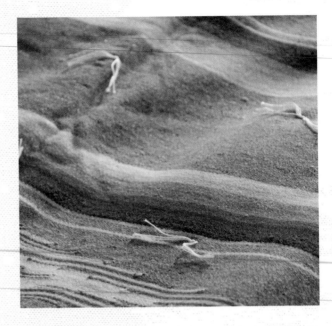

ADDITIONAL TOOLS

SEE BASIC TOOLS, PAGE 9
- Sewing-machine needle for heavyweight fabrics
- Hand-embroidery needle for quilting
- Large box of quilter's safety pins

FABRIC CUTTING INSTRUCTIONS

Cut off any fringe, hems, or binding from your blanket. Using a straight or zigzag stitch on your sewing machine, sew along the edge to keep your blanket from fraying while you are constructing your quilt.

From the vintage duck cloth, denim, or other heavyweight fabric, cut:
- Two strips, 10" [25 cm] wide by the length of your blanket

From ivory flannel and coordinating backing fabrics, we cut our 5 yards [4.6 m] of each fabric into two equal lengths, trimmed off the selvage edges, and set aside.

ASSEMBLE THE QUILT TOP

1. Referring to Diagram 1, sew the 10" [25 cm] wide fabric strips to each side of the blanket using ½" [12 mm] seam allowances. Press the seam allowances away from the blanket.

PREP FOR QUILTING

2. Sew the lengths of the backing together and do the same for the batting, if needed.

3. Prepare the Quilt Back, batting, and Quilt Top for quilting, according to Layering a Quilt Sandwich (page 22).

4. Using a ruler and beginning in the center of the Quilt Sandwich, Safety Pin Baste (page 23) the layers together in a 6" [15 cm] grid across the blanket portion of the Quilt Top only. Pin within 1" [2.5 cm] from the sides of the blanket edges and within 6" [15 cm] of the top and bottom edges.

QUILTING METHOD

5. Using two strands of ivory cotton embroidery thread and needle, tie the Quilt Sandwich at each safety pin of the marked grid, leaving 1½" [4 cm] long ties (see Tying the Quilt in the Quilting Methods section, page 24).

FINISHING THE QUILT EDGES

6. Referring to the Fold Finish Edge instructions (page 28), trim the Quilt Back and batting as instructed, then fold and pin the edges according to the directions.

7. Using a Single Stitch Edge, sew around the perimeter, following the instructions on page 29 to finish your quilt.

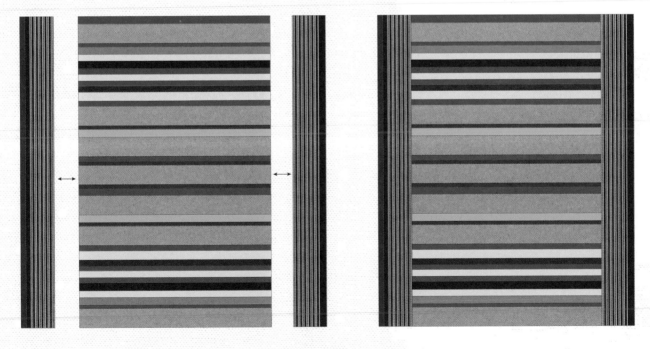

DIAGRAM 1

GRAINERY QUILT

FINISHED QUILT SIZE
Approximately 66" x 74"
[168 x 188 cm]

HOW TOUGH?
●○○○○

I'm always seeing fantastic grain, feed, seed, and flour sacks at vintage shows, with rustic stamps, stock numbers, logos, and writing on them. I love incorporating these graphics and great textures into a quilt. The Grainery Quilt features vintage wool cornerstones and one of my Parson Gray print utility linens as the border. I also used one of my flannels for the backing. This quilt is super easy; you just need to go on the hunt for the right grain sacks. I like to read in bed and usually, by morning, the book ends up on the floor, so I figured, why not add a hand-sewn pocket on the face of the grain sack to stash it? Works for me!

GRITTY TECHNIQUES

HEAVY COFFEE STAINING: Feed sacks usually have a patina to them from age, but if you wish to give them a darker, more antique look, follow the instructions on page 17.

LIGHT SANDPAPER DISTRESSING: Follow the instructions on pages 13 to 15 to apply along the seams and edges of the finished Quilt Top.

FABRICS AND SUPPLIES

- 20" x 48" [50 x 122 cm] (or larger) unopened vintage or antique feed sack for the quilt center
  NOTE: *If you're unable to find a feed sack this size, consider sewing a few smaller feed sacks together and trim to size indicated under Fabric Cutting Instructions.*
- One feed sack, with interesting stamp or graphic for the pocket
- 2 yards [1.9 m] brown print utility linen for the border
- 1 yard [1 m] navy plaid wool or cotton flannel for border cornerstones
- 5 yards [4.6 m] navy print heavy flannel for the backing
- 5 yards [4.6 m] ivory flannel for the batting
- Coordinating cotton thread for piecing quilt together
- One small spool of cotton embroidery thread in dark gray for the pocket
- One large spool of wool embroidery thread in heather gray for quilting

ADDITIONAL TOOLS

SEE BASIC TOOLS, PAGE 9
- Sewing-machine needle for heavyweight fabrics
- Embroidery needle for pocket and quilting
- Large box of quilter's safety pins
- Tools for coffee staining (optional)
- One sheet of fine-medium grit sandpaper (optional)

FABRIC CUTTING INSTRUCTIONS

NOTE: *If you are staining the feeds sacks (page 16), be sure to perform this technique before cutting into them.*

From the large feed sack, cut along one side seam and along the bottom seam to open; trim to 38½" x 46½" [98 x 118 cm] (*If piecing smaller feed sacks together, use this measurement for the finished size.*)

From the second feed sack, fussy cut:
- One stamp or graphic image, 10" x 10½" [25 x 27 cm]

From the brown print linen, cut:
- One strip, 46½" [118 cm] x width of fabric (WOF). From the strip, cut:
  - Two A rectangles, 14½" x 46½" [37 x 118 cm]
  - Two strips, 14½" [37 cm] x WOF. From the strips, cut:
    - Two B rectangles, 14½" x 38½" [37 x 98 cm]

From the navy plaid flannel, cut:
- Two strips, 14½" [37 cm] x WOF. From the strips, cut:
  - Four C squares, 14½" x 14½" [37 x 37 cm]

From the ivory flannel and the navy print flannel, cut each into two pieces, 2½ yards [2.3 m] long; trim off selvage edges and set aside.

APPLIQUÉ THE POCKET

1. With the **wrong** side up, fold over the top edge
    of the pocket ¼" [6 mm] toward the **wrong** side
    and press with an iron. Fold the edge over again
    ¼" [6 mm] and press (see Diagram 1). Pin along
    the pressed, folded edge to prepare for hand
    stitching. Using two strands of dark gray cotton
    embroidery thread, sew the pressed fold in place
    using the Back Stitch (page 32).

2. On the left-hand side of the large feed sack, center
    and pin the pocket in place. Using coordinating
    thread, machine stitch the raw edges of the pocket
    to the large feed sack ¼" [6 mm] from the raw
    edges. Again, using two strands of dark gray cotton
    embroidery thread, hand embroider a "sloppy"
    Embroidery Stitch along the three machine-
    stitched sides of the pocket to finish. (Refer to
    the stitching shown in Diagram 1 as a guide.)

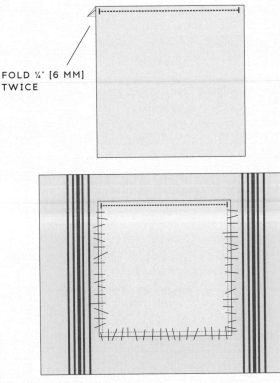

FOLD ¼" [6 MM]
TWICE

FINISHED POCKET

DIAGRAM 1

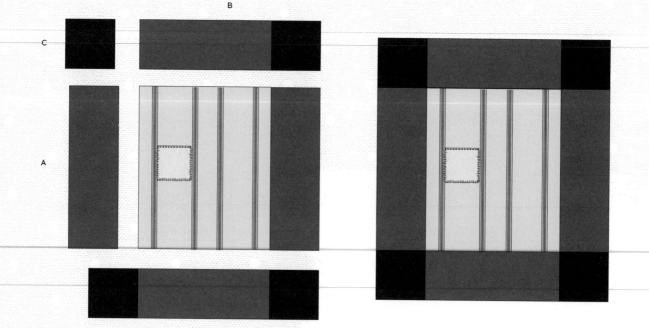

DIAGRAM 2

ASSEMBLE THE QUILT TOP

3. Referring to Diagram 2, attach the brown print A rectangles to the sides of the feed sack and press the seam allowances toward the brown print. Sew a navy plaid C square to each end of the remaining two brown print B rectangles and press the seam allowances toward the brown print. Then, attach these to the top and bottom to complete the Quilt Top. Press the seam allowances toward the brown print and set aside.

PREP FOR QUILTING

4. Sew the two lengths of ivory flannel together to use for the batting. In the same manner, sew the two lengths of navy heavy flannel together to use for the Quilt Back. Press the seams open.

5. Prepare the Quilt Back, batting, and Quilt Top for quilting, according to Layering a Quilt Sandwich (page 22).

6. Using a ruler and beginning in the center of the Quilt Sandwich, Safety Pin Baste (page 23) the layers together in a 5" [12 cm] grid across the entire Quilt Top to within 1" [2.5 cm] of the outside edge.

QUILTING METHOD

7. Using two strands of heather gray wool embroidery thread and needle, follow instructions for Tying the Quilt (page 24) at each safety pin of the marked grid and trim to 1½" [4 cm] long tails.

8. Using coordinating thread, Double Topstitch (page 25) all of the border seams, stopping the topstitching 2" to 3" [5 to 7.5 cm] from the Quilt Top edge.

FINISHING THE QUILT EDGES

9. Referring to the Fold Finish Edge (page 28), trim the Quilt Back and batting, then fold and pin the edges according to the directions.

10. Using a Double Stitch Edge (page 29), sew around the perimeter. Go back to finish stitching the Double Topstitched seams stitched in Step 8 to complete your quilt.

11. If desired, use a sheet of sandpaper to lightly sand along the seams and the outside edges of the Quilt Top to give the quilt a more distressed look.

IRON BARS QUILT

FINISHED QUILT SIZE
68" x 68" [173 x 173 cm]

HOW TOUGH?
●○○○○

The beauty in this one block quilt lies in its geometric simplicity. I based it on a vintage Amish quilt, but the contrasting ivory thread diamond quilting gives it a more contemporary feel. Yes, it looks a bit like a prison window (hence the name). Nonetheless, it's a great design that can be modified with unique colors and finished quilting techniques.

FABRICS AND SUPPLIES

- 1⅜ yards [1.3 m] rust solid for the quilt center
- 1⅜ yard [1.3 m] gray solid for the quilt center
- 3⅜ yards [3.1 m] brown solid for the border
- 4½ yards [4.2 m] ivory flannel for the batting
- 4⅜ yards [4 m] black rayon for the backing
- One spool each, ivory and black cotton embroidery thread for machine quilting

ADDITIONAL TOOLS

SEE BASIC TOOLS, PAGE 9
- Basting spray

FABRIC CUTTING INSTRUCTIONS

From the rust solid, cut one length 44½" [113 cm] x width of fabric (WOF). From the length, cut:
- Six A rectangles, 4½" x 44½" [11 x 113 cm]

From the gray solid, cut one length, 44½" [113 cm] x WOF. From the length, cut:
- Five A rectangles, 4½" x 44½" [11 x 113 cm]

From the brown solid, cut one length, 44½" [113 cm] x WOF. From the length, cut:
- Two B rectangles, 12½" x 44½" [32 x 113 cm]

From the remaining brown solid, cut one length, 8½" [174 cm] x WOF. From the length, cut:
- Two C rectangles, 12½" x 68½" [32 x 174 cm]

From the ivory flannel and the black rayon fabrics, cut each into two equal lengths; trim off the selvage edges and set aside.

ASSEMBLE THE QUILT TOP

1. Referring to Diagram 1, pin and sew the rust and gray A rectangles together to make the quilt center; press the seam allowances toward the rust fabric. Stitch the brown B rectangles to the sides of the quilt center; press the seam allowances toward the brown fabric. Sew the brown C rectangles to the top and bottom of the quilt center to complete the Quilt Top; press the seam allowances toward the brown fabric.

PREP FOR QUILTING

2. Sew the two lengths of ivory flannel together lengthwise to use for the batting. In the same manner, sew the two lengths of black rayon together lengthwise to use for the Quilt Back. Press the seams open.

3. Prepare the Quilt Top, batting, and Quilt Back for quilting, according to Layering a Quilt Sandwich (page 22). Spray Baste (page 23) the Quilt Sandwich layers together.

QUILTING METHOD

4. Using ivory embroidery thread with a stitch length of 4 on your sewing machine, follow the instructions for Straight Line Quilting (page 26) and quilt diagonal lines in an 8½" [22 cm] grid. Stitch all diagonal lines to the edges of the Quilt Top.

FINISHING THE QUILT EDGES

5. Pull the backing out of the way and trim the batting even with the edge of the Quilt Top. Next, trim the backing 3" [7.5 cm] larger than the Quilt Top and batting on all four sides.

6. Following the Self-Binding instructions on page 30, fold 2" [5 cm] of the backing fabric toward the quilt center along the right-hand side of the Quilt Top. Then, fold again to cover the ¼" [6 mm] seam allowance along the Quilt Top's edge. Topstitch in place using black thread. Repeat this step for the left side of the Quilt Top.

7. In the same manner, repeat Step 6 for the top and bottom edges to finish your quilt.

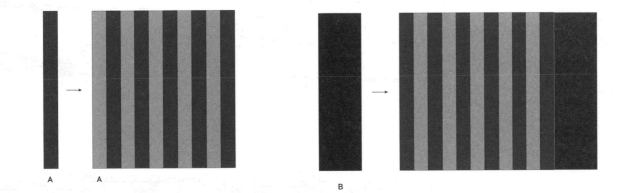

A   A

B

QUILT TOP

C

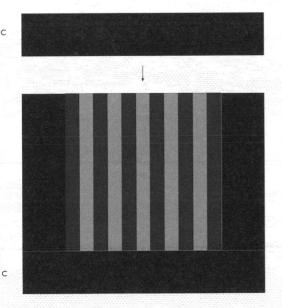

C

DIAGRAM 1

FORGED BLOCK QUILT

FINISHED QUILT SIZE
60" x 60" [152 x 152 cm]

HOW TOUGH?
●○○○○

I'm a minimalist at heart. This is a very simple design that might be one of the best first quilts to make for any beginner. The simple geometric proportions of this quilt make it perfectly okay to get creative with add-ons or wonky blocks. Cut your teeth on the clean layout and straight sewing, and for the minimalists in your life, it's a down and dirty gift of love.

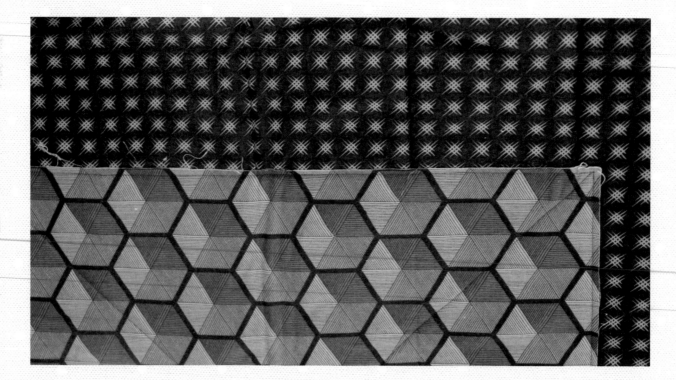

FABRICS AND SUPPLIES

- O 4 yards [3.7 m] navy print for the Quilt Top and the binding
- O 1¼ yards [1.2 m] and 1 fat quarter, blue and green print for appliqué
- O 4 yards [3.7 m] coordinating fabric for backing
- O 70" x 70" [178 x 178 cm] piece of cotton batting
- O One coordinating spool of thread for machine appliqué in dark blue

ADDITIONAL TOOLS

SEE BASIC TOOLS, PAGE 9
- O Basting spray
- O Hand-sewing needle

FABRIC CUTTING INSTRUCTIONS

From the navy print, cut:
- O Two strips, 60½" [154 cm] x width of fabric (WOF)
- O Seven strips, 2¼" [5.5 cm] x WOF

From the blue and green print yardage, cut:
- O One strip, 20" [50 cm] x WOF. From the strip, cut:
  - > One A square, 20" x 20" [50 x 50 cm]
  - > One B square, 16½" x 16½" [42 x 42 cm]
- O One strip, 16½" [42 cm] x WOF. From the strip, cut:
  - > Two B squares, 16½" x 16½" [42 x 42 cm]

From the blue and green print fat quarter, cut:
- O One B square, 16½" x 16½" [42 x 42 cm]

Cut the backing fabric into two equal lengths; trim off the selvage edges and set aside.

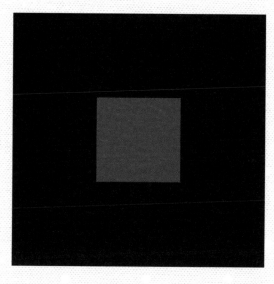

DIAGRAM 1

ASSEMBLE THE QUILT TOP

1. With the right sides together and using a ¼" [6 mm] seam allowance, pin and sew the 60½" [154 cm] navy print lengths together and press the seam open to make the base of the Quilt Top. Center the seam and trim the sides to make a 60½" x 60½" [154 x 154 cm] square.

PREP FOR QUILTING

2. Sew the two lengths of backing together to use for the Quilt Back. Press the seam open.
3. Prepare the Quilt Top, batting, and Quilt Back according to Layering a Quilt Sandwich (page 22) and follow the Spray Basting instructions (page 23).
4. Trim the batting and the Quilt Back even with the Quilt Top.

FINISHING THE QUILT EDGES

5. Make and attach the Double Fold Binding (page 26) using the navy fabric 2¼" [5.5 cm] strips.

FINISH THE QUILT

6. Fold the quilt in half vertically and finger press along the center fold. Next, open the quilt, fold it in half horizontally, and finger press.

APPLIQUÉ SQUARES, QUILTING

7. Referring to Diagram 1, fold a 20" [50 cm] blue and green print A square in half vertically and finger press it along the center fold. Repeat by folding the square in half horizontally and finger press along the fold. Flip the square over and lightly spray the **wrong** side with basting spray.
8. Using the fold marks, center the square on the Quilt Top and smooth in place.
9. Using a Straight Stitch on your sewing machine, Raw Edge Appliqué (page 31) the 20" [51 cm] square to the Quilt Top by sewing ¼" [6 mm] inside the raw edges around all four sides of the square. Then, stitch a large "X" (diagonally from corner to corner) in the center of the square to quilt the layers together.
10. Spray the **wrong** side of one 16½" [42 cm] blue and green print square and apply it to one corner of the Quilt Top, just inside the binding edge. Smooth in place and appliqué it to the Quilt Top as you did in Step 9. Continue adding the remaining three 16½" [42 cm] squares in the same manner to complete your quilt.

MARITIME QUILT

FINISHED QUILT SIZE
Approximately 68" x 77"
[173 x 196 cm]

HOW TOUGH?
●●○○○

Based on old nautical signal flags I found in an antique store, the Maritime Quilt is a great beginner project with a very basic design. We've simulated these two flags and sewed them together with an added wide border. The photo shows the original flags used as the center panels. In the instructions, you will make the same quilt without the tough reinforcement strips along the short ends of each flag (shown in tan in the photo). The coffee/tea staining on the fabrics will give you that great aged look of the originals. The binding and Triple-X tying technique complete the quilt.

GRITTY TECHNIQUES

COFFEE/TEA STAINING: Old flags are well aged from their time at sea. To give them that aged look, follow the instructions on page 17 for use on the muslin before cutting into the fabric.

DISTRESSING WITH A WIRE BRUSH: After quilt construction, follow the instructions on page 15 and use the wire brush to give the denim fabric border on the Quilt Top a well-worn look, if desired.

FABRICS AND SUPPLIES

- ⅔ yard [60 cm] red solid for flags
- 1⅛ yards [1.1 m] natural premium muslin for flags
- 1⅜ yards [1.3 m] navy solid for flags
- Three to five assorted pairs of adult-size denim and/or dark chambray pants with at least a 28" [71 cm] inseam for the border
- One adult-size black check cotton weave shirt or other dark print shirt for the border
- 5 yards [4.6 m] black linen for the backing
- 5 yards [4.6 m] black flannel for batting
- One large spool of coordinating 40-weight cotton thread for piecing
- One large spool of ivory cotton embroidery thread for tying

ADDITIONAL TOOLS

SEE BASIC TOOLS, PAGE 9
- Sewing-machine needle for heavyweight fabrics
- Hand-embroidery needle
- Tools for coffee/tea staining (optional)
- Wire brush (optional)
- Large box of quilter's safety pins

FABRIC CUTTING INSTRUCTIONS

NOTE: *If you are coffee/tea staining (page 17) the muslin yardage, be sure to perform this technique before cutting.*

From the red solid, cut two strips, 10½" [26.5 cm] x width of fabric (WOF). From strips, cut:
- One A rectangle, 10½" x 15½" [26.5 x 39 cm]
- One F rectangle, 10½" x 30½" [26.5 x 77.5 cm]

From the natural, tea-stained muslin, cut three strips, 10½" [26.5 cm] x WOF. From the strips, cut:
- Two C rectangles, 10½" x 13" [26.5 x 33 cm]
- Two D rectangles, 10½" x 35½" [26.5 x 90 cm]
- Eight E squares, 8" x 8" [20 x 20 cm]

From the navy solid, cut:
- Two strips, 8" [20 cm] x WOF. From the strips, cut:
  - Eight E squares, 8" x 8" [20 x 20 cm]
- Three strips, 10½" [26.5 cm] x WOF. From the strips, cut:
  - One B square, 10½" x 10½"[26.5 x 26.5 cm]
  - Two A rectangles, 10½" x 15½" [26.5 x 39 cm]
  - One F rectangle, 10½" x 30½" [26.5 x 77.5 cm]

From the pants, cut:
- Five legs from assorted pants. Cut each leg open along the vertical inseam and outside seam, ending with two lengths from each leg for a total of ten G strips. NOTE: *Leave the bulky seams intact for added interest to your quilt.* From these, select two matching G strips and cut both in half to make four H rectangles. Set all pant leg pieces aside for the border.

From the shirt, cut:
- Two I rectangles, approximately 10" x 12" [25 x 30.5 cm]

From the black flannel and the black linen fabrics, cut each into two equal lengths; trim off the selvage edges and set aside.

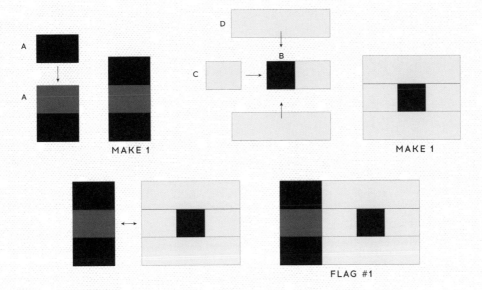

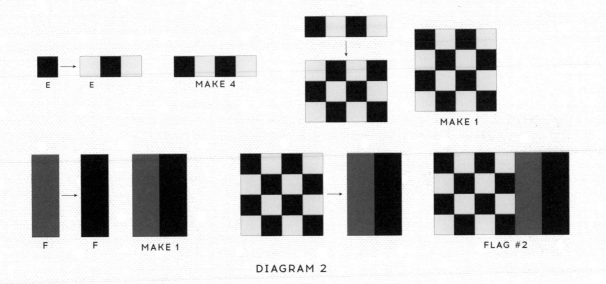

ASSEMBLE THE FLAGS

1. Referring to Diagram 1 and with right sides together, pin and sew two navy A rectangles along the long sides to one red A rectangle. Press the seam allowances toward the navy fabrics to make one red/navy A unit. In a similar manner, pin and sew two muslin C rectangles to a navy B square; press the seam allowance toward the navy fabric. Add two muslin D rectangles to top/bottom of the B/C unit; press the seam allowance toward the center. Finally, join the two units by pinning and sewing together to make Flag #1; press the seam allowance toward the navy/red.

2. Referring to Diagram 2, pin and sew two navy E squares to two muslin E squares, alternating the colors; press the seam allowance toward the navy. Make four. In a checkerboard fashion, sew the four rows together. Press the seam allowance of all of the rows in one direction.

3. Sew a red F and a navy F rectangle together along the long sides. Press toward navy. Sew the checkerboard unit to the red/navy F unit to complete Flag #2; press toward the red F.

ASSEMBLE THE QUILT TOP

3. Referring to Diagram 3, pin and sew the flags together for the quilt center. Press toward Flag #2.

4. Referring to Diagram 4, sew two assorted G pant leg strips together to make a Pieced Border Strip; press the seam open. Trim even along the bottom for a straight edge. Make four total.

5. Select two Pieced Border Strips and trim to the width of the quilt center for the top and bottom of the border. Trim the remaining two Pieced Border Strips to the length of the quilt center for the right and left sides of the border. (See Diagram 5.)

QUILT CENTER

DIAGRAM 3

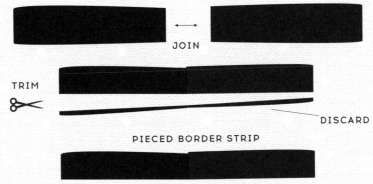

G

JOIN

TRIM

DISCARD

PIECED BORDER STRIP

MAKE 4

DIAGRAM 4

TRIM EVEN
WITH LENGTH
OF QUILT CENTER

TRIM TO WIDTH OF QUILT
CENTER

DIAGRAM 5

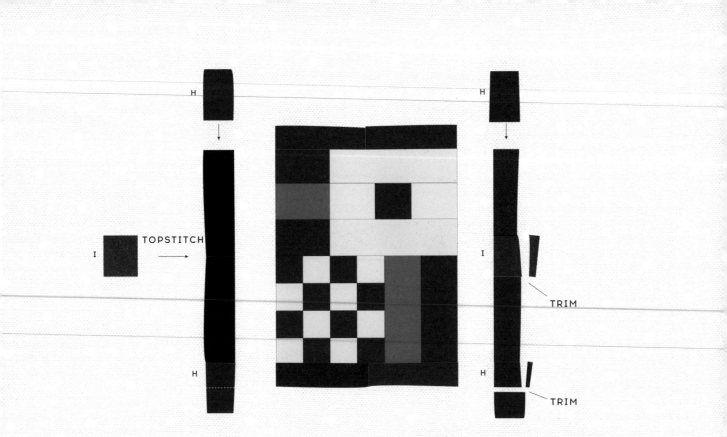

DIAGRAM 6

DIAGRAM 7

6. Referring to Diagram 6, sew top and bottom border sides to the quilt center; press the seam allowances toward the border pieces. Sew the four H pant leg rectangles to the ends of each side border, as shown. Center and trim the ends to the vertical length of the quilt center. Next, and with **right** side facing up, lay I shirt patches on the side borders, covering the middle seam; pin in place and Raw Edge Appliqué (page 31) ¼" [6 mm] from the raw edges of the patch to the border sides. Flip the pieced side border strips over and trim the excess denim from the back of the I patches to ¼" [6 mm] of the seam allowance to eliminate the bulk of fabric.

7. Referring to Diagram 7, attach the side border strips to complete the Quilt Top, then press the seam allowances toward the border strips.

PREP FOR QUILTING

8. Sew the two lengths of black flannel together lengthwise to use for the batting. In the same manner, sew the two lengths of black linen together to use for the Quilt Back. Press the seams open.

9. Prepare the Quilt Back, batting, and Quilt Top for quilting, according to Layering a Quilt Sandwich (page 22).

10. Using a ruler and beginning in the center of the Quilt Sandwich, Safety Pin Baste (page 23) the layers together in a 5" [12 cm] grid across the Quilt Top. Pin to within a few inches [5 to 7.5 cm] of the outside edges.

QUILTING METHOD

11. Using two strands of ivory cotton embroidery thread and needle, tie the Quilt Sandwich with Triple-X Hand Stitches (page 24) at each safety pin and tie at the back, trimming to ½" [12 mm] long ties.

FINISHING THE QUILT EDGES

12. Following the wonky edge of the Quilt Top, trim the Quilt Back and batting evenly and pin the edges according to the Fold Finish Edge (page 28).

13. Using two strands of ivory embroidery thread and your hand embroidery needle, sew an X-Edge Stitch (page 29) around the perimeter.

14. If desired, use a wire brush on the denim border patches surrounding the quilt center to give the quilt a worn look.

HORSE BLANKET QUILT

FINISHED QUILT SIZE
72" x 72" [183 x 183 cm]

HOW TOUGH?
●●○○○

Absolute minimalism leads to a clean, modern quilt. Another Southwest-inspired design, the Horse Blanket reflects the utilitarian beauty of simple saddle blankets from the 1800s. The proportions of the line work and the pieced background give this a well-balanced character. The piecing is fairly easy and a forgiving crop of the design allows for little mistakes to become a part of the design.

GRITTY TECHNIQUES

VERY LIGHT TEA STAINING: Before cutting the yardage, follow the instructions on page 17 to apply tea staining to the ivory solid fabric to give it a vintage look.

FABRICS AND SUPPLIES

- 1⅝ yards [1.5 m] black solid for the Quilt Top
- 4¼ yards [3.9 m] ivory solid for the Quilt Top
- 4⅝ yards [4.4 m] ivory flannel for the batting
- 4⅝ yards [4.4 m] coordinating fabric for the backing
- Coordinating spools of thread for machine quilting in ivory and black

ADDITIONAL TOOLS

SEE BASIC TOOLS, PAGE 9
- Basting spray
- Hand-sewing needle
- Tools for tea staining (optional)

FABRIC CUTTING INSTRUCTIONS

NOTE: *If you are tea staining (page 17) the ivory solid fabric, be sure to perform this technique before cutting into it.*

From the black solid, cut:
- One length, 50½" [128 cm] x width of fabric (WOF). From the length, cut:
  - Seven strips, 4½" x 50½" [11 x 128 cm]; set four I strips aside for sashing. From the remaining strips, cut:
    - Four E rectangles, 4½" x 22½" [11 x 57 cm]
    - Three D rectangles, 4½" x 14½" [11 x 37 cm]
- Two A squares, 5½" x 5½" [14 x 14 cm]
- One D rectangle, 4½" x 14½ [11 x 37 cm]
- One H square, 4½" x 4½" [11 x 11 cm]

From the ivory solid, cut:
- Two lengths, 50½" [128 cm] x WOF. From the first length, cut:
  - Two G rectangles, 14½" x 50½" [37 x 128 cm]
  - Four C rectangles, 5" x 14½" [12 x 37 cm]
- From the second length, cut:
  - Two G rectangles, 14½" x 50½" [37 x 128 cm]
  - Four B rectangles, 5" x 5½" [12 x 14 cm]
- Two lengths of fabric strips, 14½" x 45" [37 x 114 cm]. From the strips, cut:
  - Four F rectangles, 14½" x 22½" [37 x 57 cm]

From the ivory flannel and the coordinating backing fabrics, cut each into two equal lengths; trim off the selvage edges and set aside.

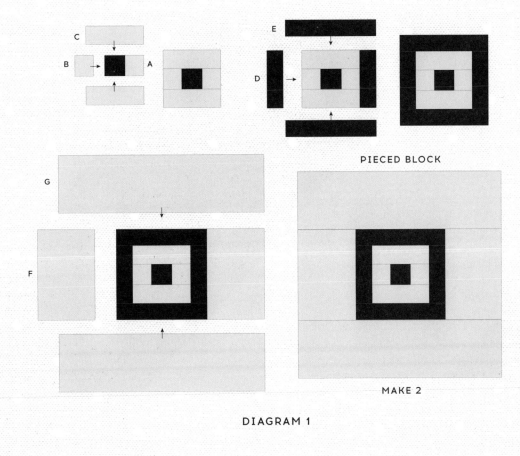

PIECED BLOCK

MAKE 2

DIAGRAM 1

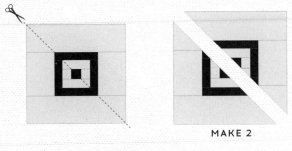

MAKE 2

DIAGRAM 2

ASSEMBLE THE PIECED BLOCKS

1. With **right** sides together, pin and sew one black A square to two ivory B rectangles (see Diagram 1); press the seam allowances toward the center. Next, sew two ivory C rectangles to the top and bottom of the A/B unit, pressing seams toward the center. Add two black D rectangles to the sides; press seams toward the black fabric. In the same manner, add two black E rectangles to the top and bottom, pressing toward black. Continue by adding two ivory F rectangles to the sides, and two ivory G rectangles to the top and bottom, pressing to complete the Pieced Block; press the seam allowance toward the black fabric. Make two total.

2. Referring to Diagram 2, fold one Pieced Block in half diagonally and finger press. With the block still folded, use your scissors to cut it in half along the fold for two Pieced Triangles. Repeat with the second block for a total of four Pieced Triangles.

DIAGRAM 3

ASSEMBLE THE QUILT TOP

3. Sew the H square, I sashing strips, and Pieced Triangles together as shown in Diagram 3. Press the seam allowance toward the center.
4. Trim the sides of the Quilt Top in a wonky fashion, according to Diagram 4, to complete the Quilt Top.

PREP FOR QUILTING

5. Sew the two lengths of ivory flannel together to use for the batting. In the same manner, sew the two lengths of backing fabric together to use for the Quilt Back. Press the seams open.
6. Prepare the Quilt Back, batting, and Quilt Top for quilting according to Layer a Quilt Sandwich (page 22) and follow the Spray Basting instructions (page 23).

QUILTING METHOD

7. Use the ivory cotton thread to Stitch-in-the-Ditch (page 26) all of the seams where the black and ivory fabrics meet. Start and stop all quilting stitches 2" to 3" [5 to 7.5 cm] from the outside edges of the Quilt Top. Continue using the ivory thread and stitch down the center of all 14½" [37 cm] wide F/G ivory fabric rectangles, pivoting at a right angle when necessary.
8. Straight Line Quilt (page 26) by sewing a cross (+) centered from top to bottom and side-to-side of the Quilt Top using black thread on the black H and I fabrics.

FINISHING THE QUILT EDGES

9. Following the wonky edge of the Quilt Top, trim the Quilt Back and the batting even and pin the edges according to the Fold Finish Edge instructions (page 28).
10. Finish the edges of the quilt, by using two strands of black thread and a hand-sewing needle, to sew the X-Edge Stitch (page 29) around the perimeter.

DIAGRAM 4

OLD GLORY QUILT

FINISHED QUILT SIZE
72" x 72" [183 x 183 cm]

HOW TOUGH?
●●○○○

This ragged version of the flag is true Americana at its best. I made the white stripes by heavily bleaching blue denim pant legs and the red stripes are repurposed from old shirts, skirts, and pants from the Salvation Army. The star field is a simple interpretation from one of my own fabrics. The edges were stitched together in a raw fashion, exposing the seams that will fray and tatter in the wash. The flag is pieced together in small sections of patchwork, so this is a relatively simple quilt for the advanced beginner.

GRITTY TECHNIQUES

HEAVY BLEACHING: The more worn and faded the denim fabric is on this quilt, the more ragged it will look. Follow the Fading Fabric instructions on page 18 to bleach the denim blue jeans after cutting.

FABRICS AND SUPPLIES

○ 1 yard [1 m] blue print for "star" section of the flag
○ Four to six red cotton knit and/or corduroy shirts/pants/skirts for the red stripes of the flag
○ Three pairs of adult-size denim blue jeans for the blue stripes of the flag
○ 4⅝ yards [4.4 m] ivory flannel for the batting
○ 4⅝ yards [4.4 m] natural muslin for the backing
○ One spool of 40 weight light gray cotton thread for piecing and quilting

ADDITIONAL TOOLS

SEE BASIC TOOLS, PAGE 9
○ Basting spray
○ Tools for bleaching (optional)
○ Design wall (optional)

FABRIC CUTTING INSTRUCTIONS

NOTE: *If you are bleaching (page 18) the denim jeans, be sure to perform this technique after cutting.*

From the blue print, cut one strip, 29½" [75 cm] x width of fabric (WOF). From the strip, cut:
○ One rectangle, 29½" x 35½" [75 x 90 cm]

From the red clothing, cut sixteen to twenty strips, approximately 5" x 24" [12 x 61 cm] long; add a few shorter length strips for interest.

From the denim blue jeans, cut long, wonky strips from the front and back legs of each, approximately 4" to 6" [10 to 15 cm] wide.
NOTE: *Keep pants pockets as part of the strips for interest, if you so desire.*

From the ivory flannel and the muslin backing yardages, cut each into two equal lengths; trim off the selvage edges and set aside.

ASSEMBLE THE QUILT TOP

1. With the **right** sides facing up, lay enough 5" [12 cm] wide red strips in a row, overlapping the ends by approximately 1" [2.5 cm], until it measures approximately 37" [94 cm] long. Pin the ends in place where they overlap. Sew the ends together using a Double Topstitch Seam (page 25). Make four strips total.

2. Following the same method as in Step 1, select and lay out enough lengths of the bleached denim strips, overlapping the ends 1" [2.5 cm], until the row measures approximately 37" [94 cm] long. Pin the ends in place where they overlap and then sew the ends together using a Double Topstitch Seam. Make three strips total.

3. Repeat Step 1 and lay out enough 5" [12 cm] wide red strips, overlapping the ends by 1" [2.5 cm], until the row measures approximately 73" [185 cm] long. Pin the ends in place where they overlap, and then sew the ends together using a Double Topstitch Seam. Make three strips total.

4. Repeat Step 1 and lay out enough of the denim strips, overlapping the ends by 1" [2.5 cm], until the row measures approximately 73" [185 cm] long. Pin the ends in place where they overlap, and then sew the ends together using a Double Topstitch Seam. Make three strips total.

TRIM   SHORT ROW UNIT

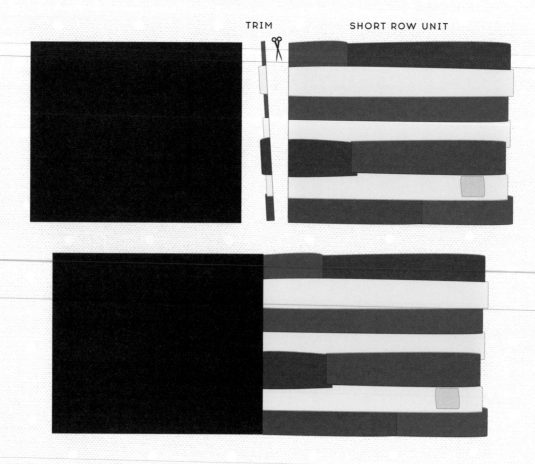

DIAGRAM 1

5. Using a design wall or a large, flat surface, lay out the blue print rectangle, the four red 37" [94 cm] strips (from Step 1), and the three denim 37" [94 cm] strips (from Step 2), according to Diagram 1. Overlap the red and denim strips up to a few inches [5 to 7.5 cm] and adjust them until the bottom red strip lines up with the bottom of the blue print rectangle. Pin the overlapping red and denim strips in place and sew the strips together using the Double Topstitch Seam to make a Short Row Unit.

6. Trim the Short Row Unit even along the left-hand side. Then, using a ½" [12 mm] seam allowance and with **right** sides together, sew the blue print rectangle to the pieced Short Row Unit. Press the seam toward the blue print rectangle.

7. Lay out the remaining three pieced denim strips and the three pieced red strips, approximately 73" [185 cm] each, as shown in Diagram 2. Continue by using the Double Topstitch Seam and piece the strips together; trim even along the left-hand side. Using the Double Topstitch Seam, sew to the bottom of the blue print Short Row Unit to complete the Quilt Top.

PREP FOR QUILTING

8. Sew the two lengths of the ivory flannel together lengthwise to use for batting. In the same manner, sew the two lengths of backing together to use for the Quilt Back. Press the seams open.

9. Prepare the Quilt Back, batting, and Quilt Top for quilting according to the Layering a Quilt Sandwich instructions on page 22, Spray Basting (page 23) the layers together.

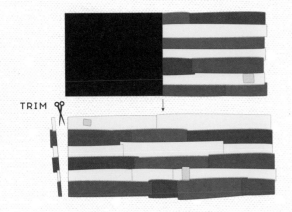

TRIM ✂

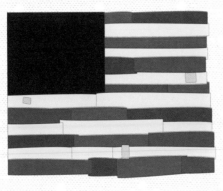

DIAGRAM 2

QUILTING METHOD

10. Use the light gray thread to Double Topstitch (page 25) the denim and red strips, horizontally and in a random fashion. Stitch to within 2" to 3" [5 to 7.5 cm] of the edge of the Quilt Top.

FINISHING THE QUILT EDGES

11. Referring to the Fold Finish Edge (page 28) instructions, trim the Quilt Back and batting even with the Quilt Top, then fold and pin the edges according to the instructions.

12. Using gray thread and a Double Stitch Edge (page 29), sew around the perimeter.

13. Go back and finish sewing your Double Stitch Quilting from Step 10 to finish the quilt.

FORT BATTERY QUILT

FINISHED QUILT SIZE
72" x 72" [183 x 183 cm]

HOW TOUGH?
●●○○○

The Fort Battery Quilt pulls from mid-century modern design, as well as American folk art. Look closely and you'll see that the layout of the radiating stripes is crooked. This effect is achieved by roughly arranging the same stripes on each side, but not having them an exact measurement. The result is a very simple but striking cascade of contrast.

FABRICS AND SUPPLIES

- 2⅛ yards [2 m] tan solid for the Quilt Top
- 1⅝ yards [1.5 m] light blue solid for the Quilt Top
- ⅔ yard [0.6 m] green linen solid for the Quilt Top
- 2⅛ yards [2 m] rust solid for the Quilt Top
- 2¼ yards [2.1 m] black solid for the Quilt Top
- 4⅝ yards [4.3 m] black flannel for the batting
- 4⅝ yards [4.3 m] coordinating fabric for the backing
- Coordinating thread for piecing
- One spool of black cotton embroidery thread for machine appliqué

ADDITIONAL TOOLS

SEE BASIC TOOLS, PAGE 9
- Basting spray

FABRIC CUTTING INSTRUCTIONS

From the tan solid, cut one length, 70¾" [180 cm] x width of fabric (WOF). From the length, cut:
- One PP rectangle, 3¾" x 70¾" [9.5 x 180 cm]
- One OO rectangle, 2¾" x 69¾" [7 x 177 cm]
- One strip, 4¾" [12 cm] x length of fabric (LOF). From the length, cut:
  > One C rectangle, 4¾" x 12¾" [12 x 32.5 cm]
  > One D rectangle, 3¾" x 14¾" [9.5 x 37.5 cm]
  > One G rectangle, 2¾"x18¾" [7 x 47.5 cm]
  > One H rectangle, 2¾"x 20¾" [7 x 52.5 cm]

From the light blue solid, cut:
- One length, 54¼" [138 cm] x WOF. From the length, cut:
  > One DD rectangle, 5¼" x 54¼" [13 x 138 cm]
  > One CC rectangle, 5¾" x 48¼" [14.5 x 123 cm]
  > One Z rectangle, 3¾" x 44¼" [9.5 x 112 cm]
  > Three strips, 3¾" [9.5 cm] x LOF. From the lengths, cut in this order:
    > One E rectangle, 3¾" x 15¾" [9.5 x 40 cm]
    > One U rectangle, 3¼" x 35¼" [8.5 x 89.5 cm]
    > One F rectangle, 3¾" x 17¾" [9.5 x 45 cm]
    > One R rectangle, 3¼" x 32¼" [8.5 x 82 cm]
    > One I rectangle, 3¾" x 20¾" [9.5 x 52.5 cm]
    > One J rectangle, 3¾" x 23¾" [9.5 x 60.5 cm]
    > One strip, 2¾" [7 cm] x LOF. From this length, cut:
      > One Q rectangle, 2¾" x 29¾" [7 x 75.5 cm]
- One V rectangle, 3¾" x 38¼" [9.5 x 97 cm]
- One Y rectangle, 3¼" x 41¼" [8.5 x 105 cm]

From the green linen, cut one strip 18" [46 cm] x WOF. From the strip, cut:
- One K rectangle, 2¼" x 23¾" [5.5 x 60.5 cm]
- One L rectangle, 2¾" x 25¼" [7 x 64 cm]

- One O rectangle, 2¼" x 27¾" [5.5 x 70.5 cm]
- One P rectangle, 2¾" x 30¼" [7 x 77 cm]
- One S rectangle, 4¼" x 32¼" [10.5 x 82 cm]
- One T rectangle, 3¾" x 35¾" [9.5 x 91 cm]

From the rust solid, cut one length, 66¼" [168 cm] x WOF. From the length, cut:
- One LL rectangle, 3¾" x 66¼" [9.5 x 168 cm]
- One KK rectangle, 4¾" x 62¼" [12 x 1.8 cm]
- One HH rectangle, 4¾" x 59¼" [12 x 150.5 cm]
- One GG rectangle, 2¾" x 56¼" [7 x 143 cm]
- One N rectangle, 2¾" x 28¾" [7 x 73 cm]
- One M rectangle, 4¼" x 25¾" [10.5 x 65.5 cm]
- Two B rectangles, 2¾" x 10¾" [7 x 27.5 cm]

From the black solid, cut:
- One length, 70¾" [178 cm] x WOF. From the length, cut:
  > One NN rectangle, 5¼" x 70¾" [13 x 178 cm]
  > One MM rectangle, 5¼" x 65¼" [13 x 166 cm]
  > One JJ rectangle, 2¾" x 62¼" [7 x 158 cm]
  > One II rectangle, 3¾" x 60¼" [9.5 x 153 cm]
  > One FF rectangle, 4¼" x 57¼" [10.5 x 145.5 cm]
  > One EE rectangle, 3¾" x 52¾" [9.5 x 134 cm]
  > One BB rectangle, 4¾" x 49¼" [12 x 125 cm]
  > One AA rectangle, 5¾" x 44¼" [14.5 x 112.5 cm]
  > One W rectangle, 4¼" x 38¼" [10.5 x 97 cm]
  > One A rectangle, 8¾" x 10¾" [22 x 27.5 cm]
- One strip, 3¾" [9.5 cm] x WOF. From the strip, cut:
  > One X rectangle, 3¾" x 41¾" [9.5 x 106 cm]

From the black flannel and the coordinating backing fabric, cut each into two equal lengths; trim off the selvage edges and set aside.

ASSEMBLE THE QUILT TOP

1. Piece the Quilt Top together in a wonky fashion. Referring to Diagram 1, and with right sides together, skew the placement of a rust B rectangle on the longer side of the A rectangle. Sew together and press the seam allowance toward A. In the same skewed manner, place the second rust B on the short side of A, as shown. Sew together and press toward A. Use your rotary cutter, ruler, and cutting mat to trim any overhang on all sides.

2. Referring to Diagram 2 (see page 80), continue piecing and trimming rectangles in a wonky fashion in alphabetical order, as shown, pressing the seam allowance toward the darker fabric to finish your Quilt Top. The outside edge of the Quilt Top will be uneven and wonky when you are finished. Trim all of the overhanging edges of the strips even, but keep the wonky, curved shape along the sides. Or, if you desire, square up the outside edge of the Quilt Top to form straight edges along the sides and right angles at the corners.

PREP FOR QUILTING

3. Sew the two lengths of the black flannel together lengthwise to use for the batting. In the same manner, sew the two lengths of the backing fabric together to use for the Quilt Back. Press the seams open.

4. Prepare the Quilt Top, batting, and Quilt Back for quilting, according to Layering a Quilt Sandwich (page 22). Spray Baste (page 23) the Quilt Sandwich layers together.

QUILTING METHOD

5. Start and stop all quilting stitches 2" to 3" [5 to 7.5 cm] from outside edges of the Quilt Top. With black embroidery thread, Stitch-in-the-Ditch (page 26) along the seams, then quilt a stitching line diagonally from the upper left corner (A) to the lower right corner (OO/PP).

FINISHING THE QUILT EDGES

6. Referring to the Fold Finish Edge (page 28), trim the Quilt Back and the batting, then fold and pin the edges according to the instructions.

7. Using the Double Stitch Edge (page 29), sew around the perimeter of the quilt. Go back and finish all of the stitching you did in Step 5 to complete your quilt.

DIAGRAM 1

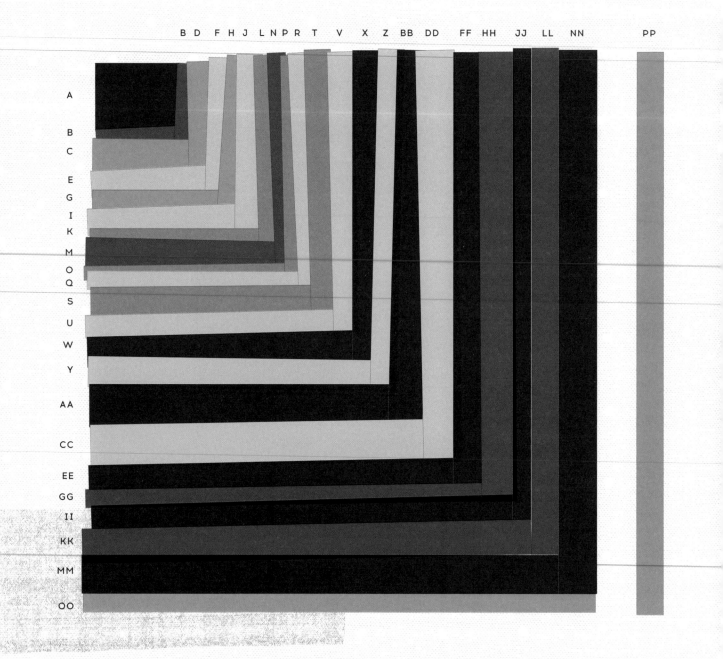

DIAGRAM 2

1890S TRADER'S QUILT

FINISHED QUILT SIZE
72" x 72" [183 x 183 cm]

HOW TOUGH?
●●●○○

Although a modern design, this quilt is loosely based on both Navajo rugs and trade blankets of the 1600s. Extremely desirable in the fur trade, woolen "point" blankets (as they were called) were marked by either weaving or dyeing point markers in one corner of the blanket based on their weight and size. Four points indicated the largest sized blankets (and closest to the size of the quilt here). In the wild, a blanket would traditionally trade for one beaver skin per point. Consider this when making one for the outdoorsman in your life. Is it a fair trade?

FABRICS AND SUPPLIES

- 4½ yards [4.2 m] ivory print utility canvas for Quilt Top
  NOTE: *We chose to use the **wrong** side of this fabric facing up as the **right** side, allowing the subtle nature of the print to show through from the back.*
- 1 yard [1 m] blue utility linen for the Quilt Top
- 1 yard [1 m] green utility linen for the Quilt Top
- 4" x 9" [10 x 23 cm] piece of each: rust print, blue stripe, cream stripe for the Quilt Top
- ⅜ yard [0.35 m] brown solid for the Quilt Top
- 4⅝ yards [4.3 m] ivory flannel for the batting
- 4⅝ yards [4.3 m] coordinating fabric for the backing
- Coordinating spools of thread for machine appliqué in blue, green, brown, and gray
- A spool of heather gray wool embroidery thread for tying

ADDITIONAL TOOLS

SEE BASIC TOOLS, PAGE 9
- Sewing-machine needle for heavyweight fabrics
- Large box of quilter's safety pins
- Hand-embroidery needle

FABRIC CUTTING INSTRUCTIONS

From the ivory print utility canvas, cut:
- Two strips, 73" [185 cm] x width of fabric (WOF)

From the blue linen and the green linen, cut each:
- One A square, 29" x 29" [74 x 74 cm]
  › Cut each square once diagonally for two triangles; discard one of each color.

From the brown solid, cut:
- Two strips, 3½" [9 cm] x WOF
- Two B rectangles, 1½" x 8½" [4 x 21.5 cm]

From each of the rust print, the blue stripe, and the cream stripe, cut:
- Two B rectangles, 1½" x 8½" [4 x 21.5 cm]

From the ivory flannel and the coordinating backing fabric, cut each into two equal lengths; trim off the selvage edges and set aside.

ASSEMBLE THE QUILT TOP

1. With the **wrong** sides together and using a ½" [12 mm] seam allowance, pin and sew the ivory utility canvas lengths together; press the seam open.

2. With the seam centered on the pieced, utility canvas Quilt Top, trim the sides so the Quilt Top measures 73" [185 cm] square.

3. With the Quilt Top seam positioned vertically, fold it in half horizontally and finger press along the fold; open the Quilt Top. Using the center seam and the finger-pressed fold as a guide, place one blue and one green triangle as shown in Diagram 1. Pin in place around the perimeter of both triangles.

DIAGRAM 1

4. With coordinating thread, use the Raw Edge Appliqué technique (page 31) and topstitch a scant ¼" [6 mm] around the inside raw edge of each triangle to secure them to the Quilt Top.

5. Next, piece together the 3½" [9 cm] x WOF brown solid strips. With the right side facing up, pin the strip to the right-hand vertical edge of the Quilt Top and, as with the center triangles, topstitch a scant ¼" [6 mm] along the left-hand vertical length of the pieced strip. Under each appliqué, triangle, and brown pieced strip, trim away the utility canvas to within ¼" [6 mm] of the seam at the back of the Quilt Top, to alleviate fabric bulk.

6. Again referring to Diagram 1 (see page 85), lay out assorted B rectangles as shown, starting 5" [12 cm] from the left vertical edge of the Quilt Top, and pin in place, spacing the pieces 1¼" [3 cm] apart. With the coordinating thread, topstitch ⅛" [3 mm] around the inside raw edge of each rectangle.

PREP FOR QUILTING

7. Sew the two lengths of ivory flannel together to use for the batting. In the same manner, sew the two lengths of backing fabric together to use for the Quilt Back. Press the seams open.

8. Prepare the Quilt Top, batting, and Quilt Back for quilting according to the Layering a Quilt Sandwich instructions on page 22.

9. Using a ruler and beginning in the center of your Quilt Sandwich, Safety Pin Baste (page 23) the layers together in a 6" [15 cm] grid across the Quilt Top. Pin to within 6" [15 cm] of the outside edges.

QUILTING METHOD

10. Using two strands of heather gray wool embroidery thread and needle, follow the Tying the Quilt instructions (page 24) at each safety pin, leaving 2" [5 cm] long ties.

FINISHING THE QUILT EDGES

11. Referring to the Fold Finish Edge instructions on page 28, trim the Quilt Back and batting, then fold and pin the edges according to the instructions.

12. Using gray thread and a Double Stitch Edge (page 29), sew around the perimeter to finish the quilt.

BEAR PAW QUILT

FINISHED QUILT SIZE
72" x 72" [183 x 183 cm]

HOW TOUGH?
●●●○○

A great folk art character and a peculiar crop takes this somewhat standard motif to a different place. I found a similar design in Anchorage, Alaska, while I was traveling, and it spawned this idea. This quilt can get very, very loose in its layout and, actually, that's the idea. If you study it, you'll see the inherent wonkiness of the pattern pieces and design. It's meant to go a bit astray. The Bear Paw Quilt works very well with tons of distressing and staining, but I kept this one fairly clean to allow the design to take center stage.

FABRICS AND SUPPLIES

- 5⅜ yards [5 m] black solid for the blocks
- 2⅜ yards [2.2 m] gray solid for the blocks
- 2⅛ yards [2 m] brown solid for the blocks
- 1⅞ yards [1.8 m] ivory solid for the appliqué
- ⅔ yard [0.6 m] rust solid for the appliqué
- 4⅝ yards [4.3 m] black flannel for the batting
- 4⅝ yards [4.3 m] coordinating fabric for backing
- 4¼ yards [3.9 m] paper-backed fusible web
- Coordinating thread for piecing
- One spool each 40 weight ivory and rust cotton thread for machine appliqué

ADDITIONAL TOOLS

SEE BASIC TOOLS, PAGE 9
- Basting spray
- One sheet of poster board 22" x 28" [55 x 70 cm]
- Marking pencil
- Design wall (optional)

TEMPLATE CUTTING INSTRUCTIONS

Cut the Bear Paw Template from the template sheet enclosed in the envelope at the front of this book. Trace the template onto poster board and label it with the seam allowance and grain line; cut the template from the poster board and set aside.

FABRIC CUTTING INSTRUCTIONS

From the black solid, cut eight strips, 23½" [60 cm] x width of fabric (WOF). From the strips, cut:

- Eight A squares, 23½" x 23½" [60 x 60 cm]

From the gray solid, cut:

- Two strips, 23½" [60 cm] x WOF. From the strips, cut:
  - Two squares, 23½" x 23½" [60 x 60 cm]
- Two strips, 17" [43 cm] x WOF. From the strips, cut:
  - Three squares, 17" x 17" [43 x 43 cm]
    - Cut each square once diagonally for six triangles

From the brown solid, cut three strips, 23½" [60 cm] x WOF. From the strips, cut:

- Three squares, 23½" x 23½" [60 x 60 cm]
- One square, 5" x 5" [12 x 12 cm]
- Cut the square once diagonally for two triangles

From the paper-backed fusible web, cut:

- One strip, 10" x 17" [25 x 43 cm] (width of fusible yardage). From this strip, subcut:
  - Two rectangles, 3½" x 10" [9 x 25 cm]

From the remaining fusible yardage, trace the Bear Paw Template 24 times onto the paper side of the fusible web; trim the shapes from the fusible web.

From the black flannel and coordinating backing fabrics, cut each into two equal lengths; trim off the selvage edges and set aside.

ASSEMBLE THE BLOCKS

1. Following the manufacuturer's instructions for the paper-backed fusible web, and referring to the Raw Edge Appliqué method (page 31), press the two fusible web D rectangles and seventeen of the bear paw shapes onto the **wrong** side of the ivory solid fabric. Cut the fused rectangles and bear paw shapes from the fabric and set aside.

2. As you did in Step 1, press the remaining seven fusible bear paw shapes onto the **wrong** side of the rust solid fabric. Cut the fused bear paw shapes from the fabric and set aside.

3. Remove the paper backing from two of the ivory bear paw shapes. Place them onto the **right** side of a black A square, according to Diagram 1, and press in place. Make three total. Repeat this process to make the remaining blocks, following the fabric color and amounts, as shown in Diagram 1.

ASSEMBLE THE QUILT TOP

4. Using a Design Wall (page 164) or other large, flat surface, lay out the blocks, large squares, and triangles according to Diagram 2.

5. Sew the blocks, squares, and triangles into rows, pressing the seam allowances in alternating directions for each row. Sew the rows together, pressing the seam to one side. Trim to square up, as shown in Diagram 3, to finish the Quilt Top.

PREP FOR QUILTING

6. Sew the two lengths of black flannel together lengthwise to use for the batting. In the same manner, sew the two lengths of backing together to use for the Quilt Back. Press the seams open.

7. Prepare the Quilt Back, batting, and Quilt Top for quilting according to the Layering a Quilt Sandwich instructions on page 22, Spray Basting (page 23) the layers together.

QUILTING METHOD

8. Stitch-in-the-Ditch (page 26) all of the diagonal seams, starting and stopping 2" to 3" [5 to 7.5 cm] from the edges of the Quilt Top. Then, using coordinating thread and a straight stitch on your sewing machine, Raw Edge Appliqué (page 31) a scant ¼" [6 mm] inside all of the bear paw shapes and ivory rectangles, pivoting where needed and stopping 2" to 3" [5 to 7.5 cm] from the edges of the Quilt Top.

FINISHING THE QUILT EDGES

9. Referring to the Fold Finish Edge (page 28), trim the Quilt Back and the batting, then fold and pin the edges according to the instructions.

10. Using coordinating thread and a Single Stitch Edge (page 29), sew around the perimeter.

11. Go back and finish the few inches of the Stitch-in-the-Ditch quilting and Raw Edge Appliqué from Step 8 to finish the quilt.

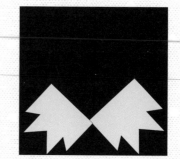

MAKE 3

MAKE 2

MAKE 1

MAKE 1

MAKE 1

MAKE 1

DIAGRAM 1

DIAGRAM 2

DIAGRAM 3

WORLD'S FAIR QUILT

FINISHED QUILT SIZE
76" x 76" [193 x 193 cm]

**FINISHED FLAG
BLOCKS SIZE**
12" x 18" [30.5 x 46 cm]

HOW TOUGH?
●●●○○

I developed a sewing pattern that featured all of these basic world flags as pennants. I had so many requests for this quilt that I had to include it here. I've used some of my own print fabrics to give this one a unified feel. It's not very tough to assemble, and it's quite fun to make.

FABRICS AND SUPPLIES

- 3⅔ to 4⅛ yards [3.4 to 3.8 m] assorted light prints in white, gray, and ivory for the blocks and appliqué
- 4¾ to 5½ yards [4.4 to 5.1 m] assorted medium to dark prints in gray, orange, blue, and gold for blocks and appliqué
- 2¼ yards [2.1 m] navy print for borders
- 7¼ yards [6.7 m] ivory flannel for batting
- 7¼ yards [6.7 m] black solid for backing
- Coordinating spools of thread for machine appliqué and piecing in dark gray, ivory, light gray, orange, blue, and gold

ADDITIONAL TOOLS

SEE BASIC TOOLS, PAGE 9

- Two sheets of poster board, 22" x 28" [55 x 70 cm]
- Design wall (optional)
- Hand-sewing needle
- Marking pencil
- Spray adhesive

TEMPLATE CUTTING INSTRUCTIONS

Cut the following templates from the template sheet enclosed in the envelope at the front of this book. Trace the templates onto poster board and label each, including seam allowances and grain lines; cut the templates from the poster board and set aside:

- Swiss Cross Flag
- English Cross Flag
- Japanese Circle Flag
- Square Flag
- Star Flag

FABRIC CUTTING INSTRUCTIONS

From the assorted light prints, cut:
- Twelve A rectangles, 12½" x 18½" [32 x 47 cm]
- Three B rectangles, 9½" x 12½" [24 x 32 cm]
- Three C rectangles, 6½" x 18½" [16.5 x 47 cm]
- One D rectangle, 6" x 12½" [15 x 32 cm]

Using your marking pencil, trace the following templates onto the **wrong** side of the remaining assorted light fabric prints and cut:
- One English Cross appliqué patch
- One set of Union Jack appliqué patches

From the assorted medium to dark prints, cut:
- Six A rectangles, 12½" x 18½" [32 x 47 cm]
- Three B rectangles, 9½" x 12½" [24 x 32 cm]
- Three C rectangles, 6½" x 18½" [16.5 x 47 cm]
- Two D rectangles, 6" x 12½" [15 x 32 cm]
- Three E rectangles, 3" x 18½" [7.5 x 47 cm]

Using your marking pencil, trace the following templates onto the **wrong** side of the remaining assorted medium to dark fabric prints and cut:
- Three Swiss Cross Flag appliqué patches
- Two English Cross Flag appliqué patches
- Three Japanese Circle Flag appliqué patches
- Two Union Jack Flag appliqué patches
- Three Square appliqué patches
- Two Star appliqué patches

From the navy print length of fabric, cut:
- Two strips, 2½" x 72½" [6 x 184 cm]
- Two strips, 2½" x 76½" [6 x 194 cm]

From the ivory flannel and the black solid yardage, cut each into three equal lengths; trim off the selvage edges and set aside.

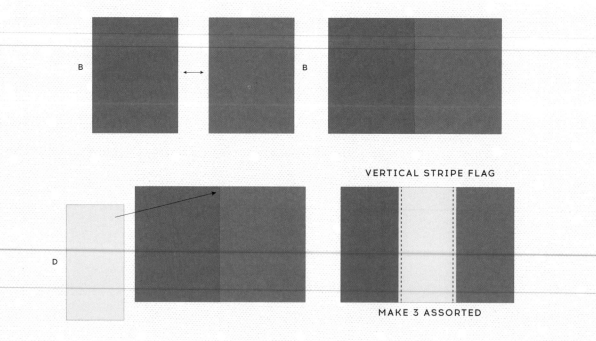

B   ↔   B

VERTICAL STRIPE FLAG

D

MAKE 3 ASSORTED

DIAGRAM 1

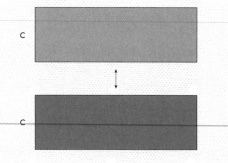

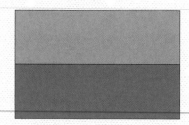

C

C

HORIZONTAL STRIPE FLAG

E

MAKE 3 ASSORTED

DIAGRAM 2

ASSEMBLE THE PIECED FLAGS

NOTE: *All appliqué pieces are sewn in place using the Raw Edge Appliqué method (page 31).*

1. Referring to Diagram 1 and with **right** sides together, pin and sew two assorted B rectangles together to make a unit; press the seam open. Center an assorted D rectangle on top of the unit with the **right** side up. Using the Raw Edge Appliqué method (page 31), pin and topstitch a ¼" [6 mm] seam allowance along the vertical raw edges and trim the excess B fabric from the back of D to finish the Vertical Stripe Flag block. Make three assorted.

2. In a similar manner, sew two assorted C rectangles together according to Diagram 2 to make a unit; press the seam open. Center an assorted E rectangle on top of the unit with the **right** side up. Pin and topstitch a ¼" [6 mm] seam allowance along both inside horizontal raw edges, trimming the excess C fabric from the back of E to finish the Horizontal Stripe Flag block. Make three assorted.

ASSEMBLE THE APPLIQUÉ FLAGS

3. Referring to Diagram 3 and using the Raw Edge Appliqué method (page 31), center a Swiss Cross Flag Appliqué patch on top of an assorted A rectangle; pin in place. Topstitch ¼" [6 mm] around the inside edge of the shape and cut the excess A fabric from the bulk of the Swiss Cross to make the Swiss Cross Flag block. Make three assorted.

4. In the same manner, center an English Cross Flag Appliqué patch on top of an assorted A rectangle; pin in place. Topstitch ¼" [6 mm] around the inside edge of the shape and cut the excess A fabric from the bulk of the English Cross to make the English Cross Flag block. Make three assorted.

5. Using the same method, make three assorted each: Japanese Circle Flag block, Union Jack Flag block, Square Flag block, and Star Flag block.

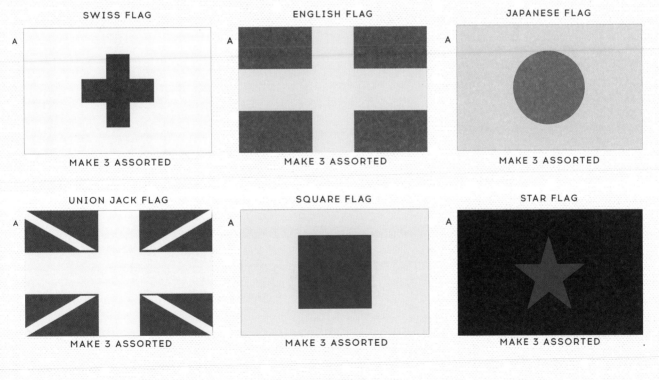

DIAGRAM 3

DIAGRAM 4

ASSEMBLE THE QUILT TOP

6. Using a Design Wall (page 164) or other flat surface, lay out six rows of four blocks each, according to Diagram 4. Sew the blocks together into rows; press the seam allowances in alternating directions for each row. Sew the rows together to make the center of the quilt; press the seam allowances in one direction.

7. Sew the navy print 2½" x 72½" [6 x 184 cm] strips to the sides of the Quilt Top; press toward the navy print. Add the remaining 2½" x 76½" [6 x 194 cm] strips to the top and bottom of the Quilt Top; press toward the navy print to finish the Quilt Top.

PREP FOR QUILTING

8. Sew the three lengths of ivory flannel together lengthwise to use for the batting. In the same manner, sew the three lengths of black solid together to use for the Quilt Back. Press the seams open.

9. Prepare the Quilt Top, batting, and Quilt Back for quilting, according to Layering a Quilt Sandwich (page 22), Spray Basting (page 23) the layers together.

QUILTING METHOD

10. Start and stop all quilting stitches 2" to 3" [5 to 7.5 cm] from the outside edges of the Quilt Top using the Stitch-in-the-Ditch (page 26) method of quilting.

FINISHING THE QUILT EDGES

11. Referring to the Fold Finish Edge (page 28), trim the Quilt Back and the batting, then fold and pin the edges according to the instructions.

12. Using coordinating thread and a Double Stitch Edge (page 29), sew around the perimeter. Go back and finish the Stitch-in-the-Ditch stitching you did in Step 10 to complete the quilt.

SKELETON CREW QUILT

FINISHED QUILT SIZE
72" x 72" [183 x 183 cm]

HOW TOUGH?
●●●●○

For the hard-to-please preteen, college-bound kid, or perhaps that pirate-loving friend you have, the Skeleton Crew Quilt is based on some of my favorite vintage graphics. To start this one, you'll want to use the graphics that I've included in this book. For the text graphics, you can either digitally scan and print or copy them directly onto Colorfast Fabric Sheets. For the skull and crossbones, you'll cut out the graphics and use them as a template. The background is made of a patchwork of vintage dark blue and black denim.

GRITTY TECHNIQUES

COFFEE STAINING: Follow the instructions on page 17 to use on the muslin yardage, for the skull, crossbones, and graphics, **before** cutting the fabric, and on the printer sheets **after** printing.

PAINT STAINING: Follow the instructions on page 19 to use on the denim before cutting to give these pieces a worn, used look.

LIGHT SANDPAPER DISTRESSING: Follow the instructions on page 15 to apply on appliqués, surface fabric, and edges of the quilt after construction.

FABRICS AND SUPPLIES

- 3 yards [2.74 m] medium blue denim for the Quilt Top
- 3 yards [2.74 m] dark blue denim for the Quilt Top
- 1½ yards [1.4 m] natural muslin for appliqué
- 4⅝ yards [4.3 m] black flannel for the batting
- 4⅝ yards [4.3 m] black print for the backing
- 3 yards [2.74 m] paper-backed fusible web
- Coordinating thread for piecing
- One spool each of black and ivory cotton embroidery thread, for hand appliqué
- One package white Colorfast Fabric Sheets by June Taylor, 8½" x 11" [21.6 x 28 cm]

ADDITIONAL TOOLS

SEE BASIC TOOLS, PAGE 9
- Sewing-machine needle for heavyweight fabrics
- A large box of quilter's safety pins (optional)
- Hand-embroidery sewing needle
- Three sheets of poster board, 22" x 28" [55 x 70 cm]
- Marking pencil
- Ink-jet printer
- Tools for coffee staining text graphics
- Tools for paint staining muslin and text graphics
- One sheet of coarse-grit sandpaper (optional)

TEMPLATE CUTTING INSTRUCTIONS

Cut the following templates from the sheet enclosed in the envelope at the front of this book.
- Skeleton Crew Template A — Defender
- Skeleton Crew Template B — 4th Co and US No. 1754
- Skeleton Crew Template C
- Skeleton Crew Template D
- Skeleton Crew Template E
- Skeleton Crew Template F

Trace Templates C through F onto poster board and label each template, including grain lines; cut the templates from the poster board and set aside.

PRINT TEXT GRAPHICS

Photocopy Templates A and B onto the Colorfast
Fabric Sheets and heat set images according to the
manufacturer's instructions and peel off backing
before staining.

STAIN MUSLIN YARDAGE AND
PRINTED FABRIC SHEETS

Coffee stain (page 17) the muslin yardage and Fabric
Sheets (with the printed text graphics). Allow to dry
completely and press.

Lightly paint stain (page 19) the coffee-stained
muslin yardage and Fabric Sheets (with the printed
text graphics). Allow to dry completely and press.

DYE DENIM YARDAGES

Dye (page 19) the denim yardages for added visual
texture. Allow to dry completely and press.

FABRIC CUTTING INSTRUCTIONS

NOTE: *Be sure to stain the muslin yardage and printed
fabric sheets and dye the denim yardage before cutting
into the fabrics.*

From the medium and dark blue denim, cut a variety
of large patches for the Quilt Top. Approximate cut
sizes for the top (left to right, top to bottom), are as
follows:

From the medium blue denim, cut one piece, each:
- O 20" x 26" [50 x 66 cm]
- O 28" x 30" [71 x 76 cm]
- O 26" x 27" [66 x 68.5 cm]
- O 10" x 26" [25 x 66 cm]
- O 28" x 36" [71 x 91 cm]

From the dark blue denim, cut one piece, each:
- O 20" x 48" [50 x 122 cm]
- O 30" x 48" [76 x 122 cm]
- O 20" x 28" [50 x 71 cm]

From the black flannel and the black print backing
yardage, cut each into two equal lengths; trim off the
selvage edges and set aside.

PREPARE FOR APPLIQUÉ

1. Cut 2 pieces of paper-backed fusible web 8½" x 11" [21.6 x 28 cm]. Place your printed and stained Template A fabric sheet facing down (**wrong** side facing up) on your ironing board. Lay the fusible side of a fusible web sheet onto the **wrong** side of the fabric and press according to the manufacturer's instructions; set aside to cool. Once finished ironing and cooling the fusible web sheets, cut Templates A and B along the edges, then cut Template B in half to separate the two phrases; set aside.

2. Place poster board Template C **wrong** side up and trace onto the paper side of the fusible web yardage. Cut the shape from the fusible web, and set aside. In the same manner, trace and cut Templates D and E; set aside.

3. With the **wrong** side of the muslin yardage facing up, place the fusible shapes (Templates C through F) on the muslin with the paper side up; press the shapes onto the muslin with the iron according to the manufacturer's instructions; set aside to cool. Cut out each shape and set aside.

   TIP: *Look for unusual staining on the **right** side of the muslin to place the shapes on top of. This will add interest to the finished Quilt Top.*

ASSEMBLE THE QUILT TOP

4. Referring to Diagram 1 and using a large, flat surface, overlap all of the raw-edge denim pieces to make an approximate 73" x 73" [185 x 185 cm] Quilt Top. Making sure there is at least a 1" [2.5 cm] overlap, pin the denim pieces together to prepare for sewing. Topstitch the pieces together, stitching approximately ⅜" [1 cm] away from the raw edges and backstitching at each end to make the Quilt Top base. Trim to a 73" [185 cm] square, if needed.

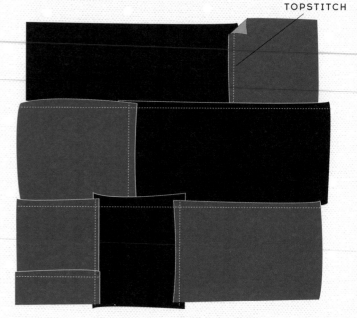

TOPSTITCH

PIECED QUILT TOP

DIAGRAM 1

5. Fold and finger press the Quilt Top in half both horizontally and vertically. Remove the paper backing from the fused appliqué shapes. Using the finger-pressed lines and flat image of the Quilt Top as a guide, lay out the appliqués vertically and fuse in place with an iron according to the manufacturer's instructions. Using black cotton embroidery thread, hand stitch large Running Stitches (page 33) a scant ¼" [6 mm] from the raw edges around all shapes except for the stars. Using the same technique, hand stitch Running Stitches around the edges of the stars with ivory cotton embroidery thread.

PREP FOR QUILTING

6. Sew the two lengths of black flannel together lengthwise to use for batting. In the same manner, sew the two lengths of black print backing together to use for the Quilt Back. Press the seams open.

7. Prepare the Quilt Back, batting, and Quilt Top for quilting, according to Layering a Quilt Sandwich on page 22.

8. Using a ruler and beginning in the center of the Quilt Sandwich, Safety Pin Baste (page 23) the layers together in a 6" [15 cm] grid across the Quilt Top. Pin to within 6" [15 cm] of the outside edges.

QUILTING METHOD

9. Using two strands of ivory cotton embroidery thread and needle, tie the Quilt Sandwich by Double-X Cross Stitching (page 33) at each safety pin, leaving ½" [12 mm] long ties.

FINISHING THE QUILT EDGES

10. Referring to the Fold Finish Edge (page 28), trim the Quilt Back and the batting, then fold and pin the edges according to the instructions.

11. Finish the edges of the quilt by using two strands of ivory embroidery thread and needle, and hand sew the X-Edge Stitch (page 29) around the perimeter.

12. If desired, use sandpaper and lightly sand along the seams and the outside edges of the Quilt Top to give the quilt a more distressed look.

PAINTED DESERT QUILT

FINISHED QUILT SIZE
72" x 72" [183 x 183 cm]

HOW TOUGH?
●●●●○

Directly inspired by Navajo weavings that I discovered in my travels to Arizona, the Painted Desert Quilt has beautiful simplicity. The symmetry of the geometric pattern captures the true affection I have for design rooted in spirit and honor. It takes a bit of time and patience to get these larger pieces in good order, but the results are striking.

FABRICS AND SUPPLIES

- O 4 yards [3.7 m] ivory solid for the Quilt Top
- O 2⅔ yards [2.5 m] black solid for the Quilt Top
- O ¾ yard [0.7 m] rust solid for the Quilt Top
- O 2" x 9" [5 x 23 cm] piece of each: rust print, blue print, brown print, ivory print
- O 4⅝ yards [4.3 m] ivory flannel for the batting
- O 4⅝ yards [4.3 m] coordinating fabric for the backing
- O Coordinating thread for piecing
- O One spool of each 40 weight black and rust cotton thread for quilting
- O One spool of heather gray wool embroidery thread

ADDITIONAL TOOLS

SEE BASIC TOOLS, PAGE 9
- O Freezer paper
- O Basting spray
- O Hand-sewing needle
- O Large box of quilter's safety pins (optional)

FABRIC CUTTING INSTRUCTIONS

From the ivory solid, cut:
- O One length of fabric (LOF) strip, 73" [185 cm] x width of fabric (WOF). From the length, cut:
  - › Two N strips, 3¼" [8.5 cm] x LOF
  - › Four strips, 7" [17 cm] x LOF. From two strips, cut:
    - › Four A rectangles, 7" x 31¾" [17 x 80.5 cm]
  - › From one strip, cut:
    - › Three C rectangles, 7" x 22¾" [17 x 58 cm]
  - › From one strip, cut:
    - › One C rectangle, 7" x 22¾" [17 x 58 cm]
    - › Three E rectangles, 7" x 16¼" [17 x 41.5 cm]

From the remaining ivory solid yardage, cut:
- O One strip, 16" [40.5 cm] x WOF. From the strip, cut:
  - › One M rectangle, 16" x 28" [40.5 x 71 cm]
  - › One P square, 11½" x 11½" [29 x 29 cm]
  - › Two strips, 8¼" [21 cm] x WOF. From the strips, cut:
    - › Four L squares, 8¼" x 8¼" [21 x 21 cm]
    - › Four H rectangles, 7" x 8¼" [17 x 21 cm]
  - › Four strips, 7" [17 cm] x WOF. From the strips, cut:
    - › Two J rectangles, 7" x 28½" [17 x 72.5 cm]
    - › Two G rectangles, 7" x 13½" [17 x 34 cm]
    - › One E rectangle, 7" x 16¼" [17 x 41.5 cm]

From the black solid, cut:
- O One strip, 23½" [60 cm] x WOF. From the strip, cut:
  - › One O square, 20½" x 20½" [52 x 52 cm]
  - › Two B rectangles, 7" x 23½" [17 x 60 cm]
- O Ten strips, 7" [17 cm] x WOF. From two strips, cut:
  - › Two D rectangles, 7" x 41½" [17 x 105 cm]
  - › From four strips, cut:
    - › Four F rectangles, 7" x 27½" [17 x 70 cm]
  - › From four strips, cut:
    - › Four I rectangles, 7" x 29" [17 x 74 cm]

From the rust solid, cut:
- O Two K rectangles, 16" x 22¾" [40.5 x 58 cm]

From the rust print, navy print, ivory stripe, and blue print, cut each:
- O One Q rectangle, 1½" x 8½" [4 x 21.5 cm]

From the ivory flannel and the coordinating backing yardage, cut each into two equal lengths; trim off the selvage edges and set aside.

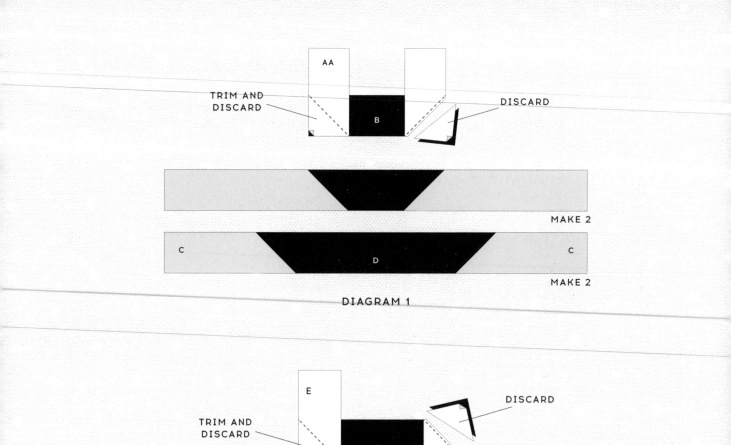

AA

TRIM AND DISCARD

DISCARD

B

MAKE 2

C   C

D

MAKE 2

DIAGRAM 1

E

TRIM AND DISCARD

DISCARD

F

G

E/F/G UNIT

MAKE 2

DIAGRAM 2

ASSEMBLE THE QUILT TOP

1. With the **right** sides together, lay two ivory solid A rectangles at right angles on each end of one black solid B rectangle (see Diagram 1). Using a ruler and marking pencil, draw diagonal lines on the A pieces, where A overlaps B. Pin and sew the A pieces to the B pieces. Trim the seam allowances to ¼" [6 mm] and press the seam allowance toward B to make an A/B Row. Make two.

2. In the same manner, lay two ivory C rectangles on each end of one black D rectangle. Mark diagonal lines, pin, sew, and trim the seam allowances. Open and press the seam allowance toward D to make a C/D Row. Make two.

3. Paying attention to orientation and with **right** sides together, lay one ivory E rectangle on the left-hand side of one black F rectangle (see Diagram 2). Then lay one ivory G rectangle on the right-hand side of the black F rectangle as shown. Draw diagonal lines, pin, sew, and trim the seam allowances. Open and press the seams toward the black F to make an E/F/G Unit. Make two.

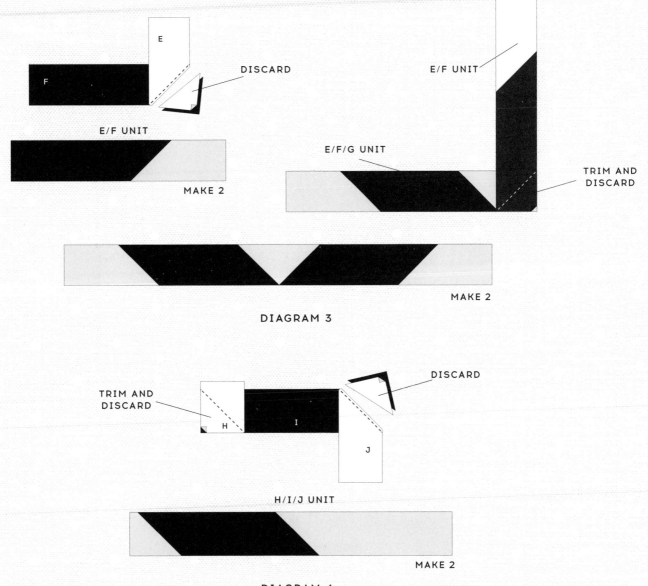

DISCARD

E/F UNIT

TRIM AND DISCARD

E/F UNIT

E/F/G UNIT

MAKE 2

MAKE 2

DIAGRAM 3

TRIM AND DISCARD

DISCARD

H/I/J UNIT

MAKE 2

DIAGRAM 4

4. In the same manner, and with **right** sides together, lay one ivory E rectangle on the right-hand side of the black F rectangle (see Diagram 3). Draw a diagonal line, pin, sew, and trim the seam allowance. Open and press toward the black F to make an E/F Unit. Make two.

5. Paying attention to the orientation and with the **right** sides together, lay the E/F Unit at a right angle on the right-hand side of the E/F/G Unit (also shown in Diagram 3). Draw a diagonal line, pin, sew, and trim the seam allowance. Open and press toward the black E/F Unit to make an E/F/G Row. Make two.

6. With **right** sides together, lay one ivory H rectangle on the left-hand side of one black I rectangle. Then lay one ivory J rectangle on the right-hand side of the I piece (see Diagram 4). Draw diagonal lines, pin, sew, and trim the seam allowances. Open and press toward the black I to make an H/I/J Unit. Make two.

7. With **right** sides together, lay one ivory H rectangle on the right-hand side of one black I rectangle (see Diagram 5). Draw a diagonal line, pin, sew, and trim the seam allowance, as shown. Open and press toward the black I to make an H/I Unit. Make two.

8. Paying attention to orientation and with **right** sides together, lay the H/I Unit on the right-hand side of the H/I/J Unit (also shown in Diagram 5). Draw a diagonal line, pin, sew, and trim the seam allowance. Open and press toward the black H/I Unit to make the H/I/J Row. Make two.

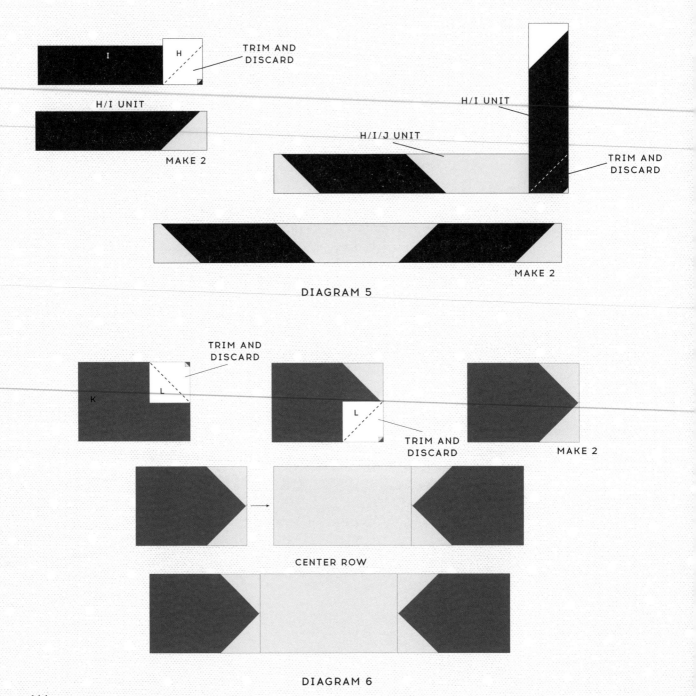

DIAGRAM 5

DIAGRAM 6

9. Draw a diagonal line on the **wrong** side of one ivory L square. With **right** sides together, place on the upper right-hand corner of the rust solid K rectangle (see Diagram 6). Pin, sew, and trim the seam allowance. Open and press toward the rust K.

10. Repeat Step 9, using an ivory L square on the lower right-hand corner of the rust K to make the K/L Unit. Make two.

11. Join the K/L Units to each end of the ivory M rectangle to complete the center row, also shown in Diagram 6. Press toward the ivory M.

12. Referring to Diagram 7, piece the rows together, as shown, pressing in one direction to make the Quilt Top.

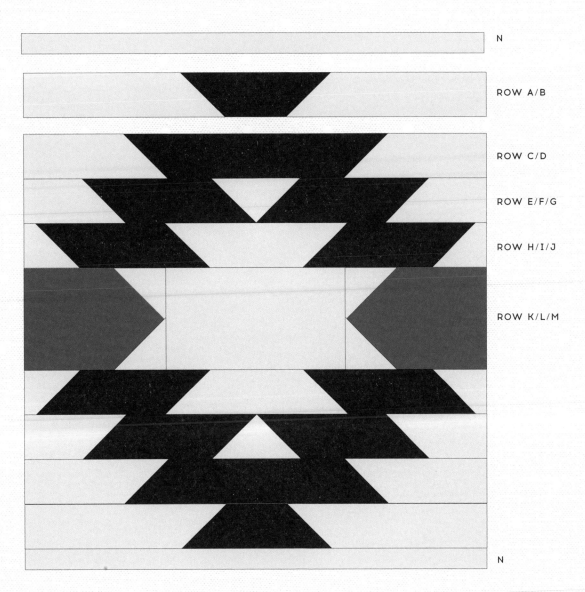

N

ROW A/B

ROW C/D

ROW E/F/G

ROW H/I/J

ROW K/L/M

N

DIAGRAM 7

DIAGRAM 8

APPLIQUÉ THE CENTER ON-POINT SQUARES AND SMALL RECTANGLES

13. Using the Freezer Paper Appliqué Method (page 31), appliqué the black O square to the quilt center (see Diagram 8) using a ⅛" [3 mm] seam. Then, trim away the Quilt Top fabric layer from the back of O to within ¼" [6 mm] of the seam. Finally, appliqué the ivory P square to the center of the O square. Trim away the O fabric layer from the back of P to within ¼" [6 mm] of the seam to finish the Quilt Top.

14. Referring to Diagram 8, lay out the assorted Q rectangles as shown on the lower left side. Place the rust Q rectangle 1½" [3.8 cm] from the left edge and ½" [12 mm] from the bottom edge. Space the remaining rectangles 1" [2.5 cm] apart and pin them in place. With a coordinating thread, Raw Edge Appliqué (page 31) the rectangles in place, topstitching ⅛" [3 mm] around the inside raw edges of each rectangle.

PREP FOR QUILTING

15. Sew the two lengths of ivory flannel together lengthwise to use for the batting. In the same manner, sew the two lengths of backing together to use for the Quilt Back. Press the seams open.

16. Prepare the Quilt Back, batting, and the Quilt Top for quilting, according to Layering a Quilt Sandwich (page 22), Spray Basting (page 23) the layers together.

QUILTING METHOD

17. Start and stop all quilting stitches 2" to 3" [5 to 7.5 cm] from the outside edges of the Quilt Top. Use the Stitch-in-the-Ditch (page 26) method of quilting along the perimeter of the black and rust fabric patches.

FINISHING THE QUILT EDGES

18. Referring to the Fold Finish Edge (page 28), trim the Quilt Back and the batting, then fold and pin the edges according to the directions.

19. Using the Double Stitch Edge (page 29), sew around the perimeter to finish the quilt.

COAL MINE QUILT

FINISHED QUILT SIZE
Approximately 67" x 72"
[170 x 183 cm]

HOW TOUGH?
●●●●●

An amazing quilt, the Coal Mine is among my favorites in the book. This is a boro quilt (boro meaning rag or ragged) and to make one is simply to eschew almost everything you might know about conventional sewing and quilting. In the utilitarian culture of Japan's peasant farmers, boro embodies their sense of profound resourcefulness and their ethic of *mottainai,* or regret of wastefulness. This is the ultimate in repurposing of materials, and a technique handed down for generations. So, in designing this quilt, I endeavored to do the same. All of the materials for this quilt were found in thrift stores. I spent very little on the materials, which include vintage shirts, jeans, and skirts in denim, cotton, and wool. The quilt uses many unique hand-sewing techniques, and you'll get to make up your own design. The pattern here is created by using scraps from your own life, and that is what makes every boro quilt different and unique.

GRITTY TECHNIQUES

INDIGO DYEING: Using indigo dyes on some of the vintage and aged denim will add a richness and depth to the quilt; vary the dyeing times for different pieces for the best results. Follow the Fabric Dyeing instructions (or the manufacturer's instructions for your chosen dye) on page 19 to apply to the assorted fabrics before construction.

LIGHT SANDPAPER DISTRESSING: Follow the instructions on page 15 to add wear and roughness to the quilt when it is finished.

FABRICS AND SUPPLIES

- Assortment of pants, jeans, and shirts in blue, gray, and black for the Quilt Top
- 4⅜ yards [4 m] hand-dyed blue linen for the backing
- 4⅜ yards [4 m] ivory flannel for the batting
- Coordinating thread for piecing
- One large spool of embroidery thread in natural

ADDITIONAL TOOLS

SEE BASIC TOOLS, PAGE 9
- Hand-embroidery needle
- Large box of quilter's safety pins (optional)
- Camera (optional)
- Tools for indigo dyeing (optional)
- One sheet of coarse-grit sandpaper (optional)

FABRIC CUTTING INSTRUCTIONS

NOTE: *If you are dyeing (page 19) the fabrics, be sure to perform this technique before cutting.*

From the clothing, cut a variety of large, medium, and small patches from the pant legs and shirts. For interest, leave in elements such as the shirt plackets, sewn seams, and pockets. Also consider splitting a pant leg along one seam and opening it for larger fabric patches.

From the ivory flannel and the blue linen yardage, cut each into two equal lengths; trim off the selvage edges and set aside.

ASSEMBLE THE QUILT TOP

1. On a large, flat surface, overlap enough large and medium-size raw-edge clothing pieces to measure approximately 68" x 73" [173 x 185 cm] (see Diagram 1), making sure there is at least a 1" [2.5 cm] overlap. Pin all of the pieces together at the overlap. Topstitch the pieces together, stitching ⅜" [1 cm] away from the raw edges and back-stitching at each end. Trim away any excess fabric from the back of the Quilt Top, leaving a ¼" [6 mm] seam allowance to alleviate bulk from your finished quilt.

NOTE: *Keep in mind that your quilt is unique and you can piece it together any way you want.*

DIAGRAM 1

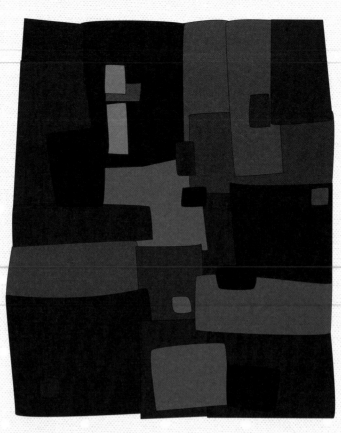

DIAGRAM 2

PREP FOR QUILTING

2. Sew the two lengths of ivory flannel together lengthwise to use for the batting. In the same manner, sew the two lengths of blue linen together to use for the Quilt Back. Press the seam open.

3. Prepare the Quilt Back, batting, and Quilt Top for quilting, according to Layering a Quilt Sandwich (page 22). Thread Baste (page 23) through all of the layers or Safety Pin Baste (page 23) the layers together.

QUILTING METHOD

4. Follow the instructions for Boro Stitching (page 33) to quilt the Quilt Sandwich. Leave 1" [2.5 cm] unstitched around the outside edges of the quilt.

   TIP: *Reverse the direction of the Boro/Running Stitches, either vertically or horizontally, in each patch for a more textured look.*

5. Once you are satisfied with how the Boro Stitches look on the large patches of your Quilt Top, randomly arrange several smaller fabric patches on the Quilt Top to your liking (see Diagram 2).

   TIP: *Take a photo for reference or pin the patches in place until you are ready to stitch them to the Quilt Top. Begin the Boro Stitches on small patches and consider adding a Blanket Stitch (page 32) to the corners of some of the patches like we did for added visual interest.*

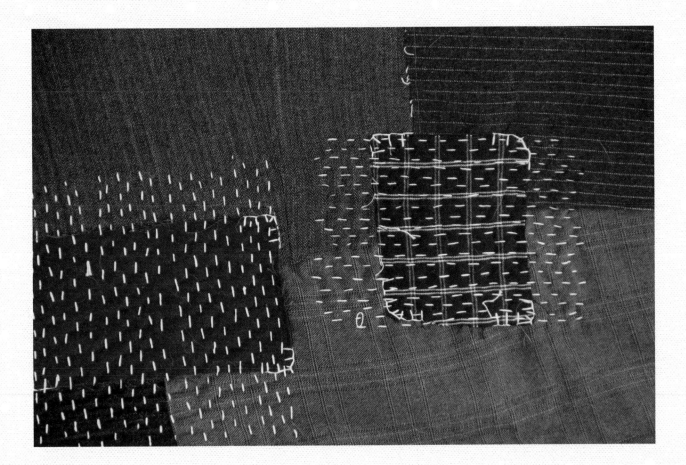

FINISHING THE QUILT EDGES

6. Referring to the Fold Finish Edge instructions (page 28), trim the Quilt Back and batting, then fold and pin the edges.

7. Using the Single Stitch Edge (page 29), sew around the perimeter to finish the quilt. Remove any Thread Basting.

8. If desired, use sandpaper to lightly sand along the surface and edges of the patches to give the quilt a more distressed look.

FALLING WIND QUILT

FINISHED QUILT SIZE
68" x 72" [173 x 183 cm]

HOW TOUGH?

It's a bit of a stretch to call this one a quilt; it's more of a throw or a coverlet. The pattern is based on my interpretation of can-can dancers, petticoats, and bustles of the 1800s. The tacking that creates the layered drapes is meant to be a bit loose, so the effect is a dramatically unrefined feel. I chose dark colors to keep it from becoming too feminine, and to create a decidedly modern feel—my ode to the women of the Wild West!

FABRICS AND SUPPLIES

- 4¼ yards [3.9 m] dark green solid* for the Quilt Top
- 4¼ yards [3.9 m] dark brown solid* for the Quilt Top
- 2⅛ yards [2 m] black solid* for the Quilt Top
- 4⅝ yards [4.3 m] black flannel for the batting
- 4⅝ yards [4.3 m] of coordinating fabric for the backing
- Coordinating thread for piecing
- Spool of black cotton embroidery thread for machine quilting

Prewash; remove immediately from clothes dryer and fold fabric until needed; do not iron.

ADDITIONAL TOOLS

SEE BASIC TOOLS, PAGE 9
- 2½" x 2½" [6 x 6 cm] square quilter's ruler
- Basting spray

FABRIC CUTTING INSTRUCTIONS

From each green and brown solid, cut:
- Two lengths, 73" [185 cm] x width of fabric (WOF)

From the black solid, cut:
- One length, 73" [185 cm] x WOF

From the black flannel and the coordinating backing fabrics, cut each into two equal lengths; trim off the selvage edges and set aside.

ASSEMBLE THE QUILT TOP: SEWING THE FLANGES

1. Using a ¼" [6 mm] seam allowance, sew together the two lengths of green solid fabric (see Diagram 1); press the seam to one side.
2. Lay the pieced fabric on a large table or other flat surface with the **right** side facing up and the seam placed horizontally. Position the 6" x 24" [15 x 61 cm] ruler on the fabric surface horizontally, lining up the 4½" x 24" [11 x 61 cm] line of the ruler with the top edge of the fabric (see Diagram 2).

   TIP: *Place a few small, heavy objects, such as paperweights, on top of the ruler to keep the ruler from shifting.*

3. Taking from the fabric yardage in front of ruler, fold the length up onto ruler to the 2" [5 cm] mark (see Diagram 3); pin the two layers at the fold and do so along the 73" [185 cm] width to complete pinning your first flange.

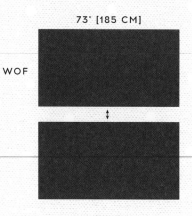

DIAGRAM 1

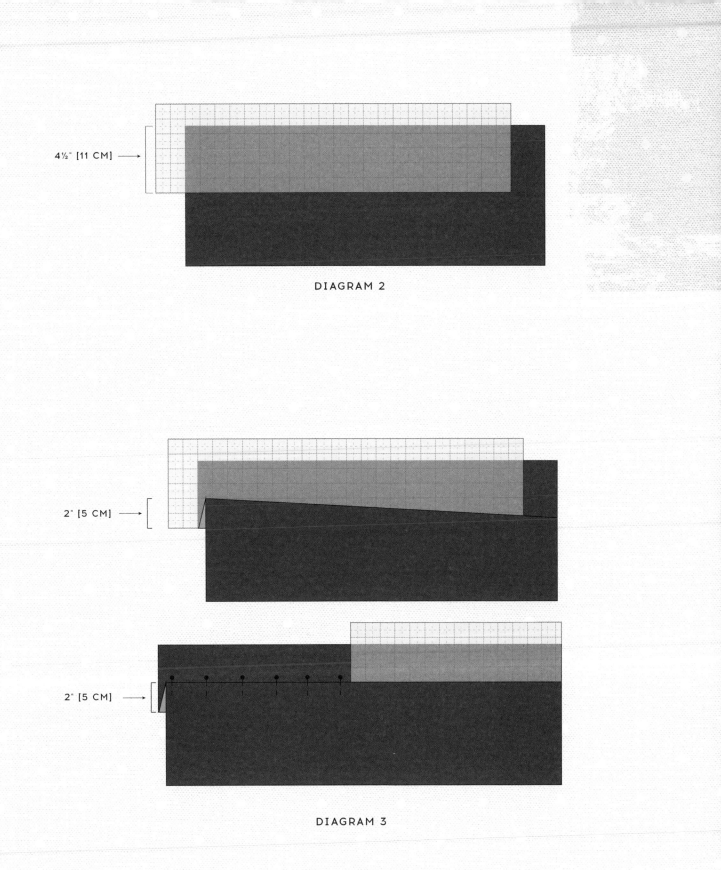

4½" [11 CM]

DIAGRAM 2

2" [5 CM]

2" [5 CM]

DIAGRAM 3

4. At the sewing machine, with the pinned fold on the right-hand side, take the 2½" x 2½" [6 x 6 cm] ruler and measure 2" [5 cm] to the left of the fold (see Diagram 4). Begin sewing at the 2" [5 cm] mark. Continue using the 2" ruler, sewing as you go, to complete your first 2" [5 cm] flange.

5. Back at your table, smooth your first flange flat as shown in Diagram 5. Place the 2" [5 cm] mark of your ruler on the fold of your first flange and repeat Steps 3 and 4 for your second flange. Continue in the same manner to make six flanges total.

6. Return to your table and flip flange #6 flat (see Diagram 6). Place the ruler's edge ¼" [6 mm] beyond the fold of flange #6 and trim the excess fabric from the width of the flanged unit with your rotary cutter on your cutting mat. Discard the excess fabric and set the unit aside.

2" [5 CM]

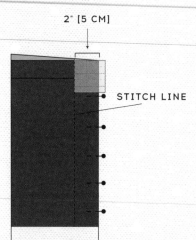

STITCH LINE

FLANGE

DIAGRAM 4

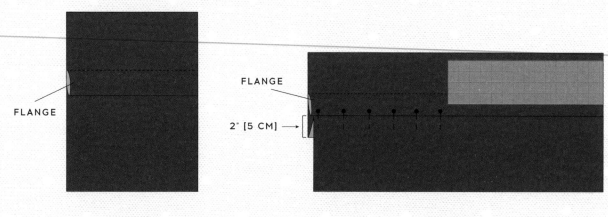

FLANGE

2" [5 CM] →

DIAGRAM 5

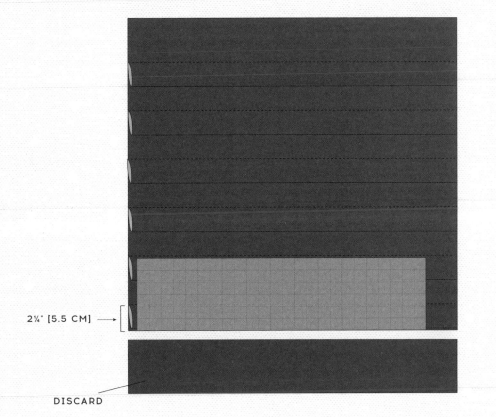

2¼" [5.5 CM] →

DISCARD

DIAGRAM 6

7. In the same manner, with the **right** side up on the table, place a long ruler along the edge of the black solid at the 2¼" [5.5 cm] mark as you did in Step 2. Make your first flange as you did in Steps 3 and 4. Make four flanges total. Place the ruler's ¼" [6 mm] mark along the fold of flange #4. Trim excess fabric from the width of the flanged unit as you did in Step 6. Discard the excess fabric and set the unit aside.

8. Sew the two lengths of brown solid together as you did in Step 1. Refer to Step 7 to make flanges; make six flanges total.

9. As you did in Step 6, flip flange #6 flat. This time, place the ruler 2½" [11 cm] from the flange fold, trim the excess fabric, and set aside.

10. Using a ¼" [6 mm] seam allowance and the **right** (flange) sides together, pin the bottom of the green unit (see Diagram 7) to the top of the black unit and sew together along the raw edge; press the seam allowance toward the black.

11. In the same manner, sew the green/black unit to the top of the brown flanged unit to complete the Quilt Top (see Diagram 8); press the seam allowance toward the black.

PREP FOR QUILTING

12. Sew the two lengths of black flannel together lengthwise to use for batting. In the same manner, sew the two lengths of the backing fabric together to use for the Quilt Back. Press the seams open.

13. Follow the Spray Basting method (page 23) for Layering a Quilt Sandwich (page 22) and layer the Quilt Top, batting, and the Quilt Back for quilting.

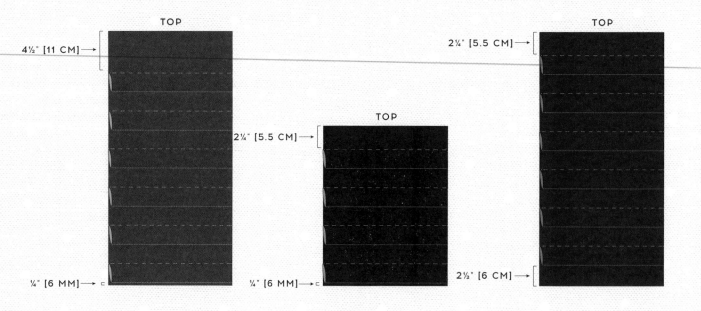

TOP

4½" [11 CM] →

¼" [6 MM] →

2¼" [5.5 CM] →

TOP

¼" [6 MM] →

2¼" [5.5 CM] →

TOP

2½" [6 CM] →

DIAGRAM 7

QUILTING METHOD

14. Smooth all the flanges in one direction toward the green solid (see Diagram 9).
15. Using the long ruler and a light-colored marking pencil, measure 12" [30.5 cm] in from the right-hand edge of the Quilt Top and mark a 12" [30.5 cm] line the entire vertical length of the Quilt Top. Flip the Quilt Top so the brown fabric is at the top. Using black embroidery thread (shown as white stitches for clarity, see Diagram 9), needle down 1" [2.5 cm] below the top edge of the Quilt Top on the drawn line at the bottom edge of the quilt, backstitch, and continue to stitch following the line, sewing the flanges flat in one direction; stop 1" [2.5 cm] from the bottom edge and backstitch. Follow the same procedure to secure the flanges along the left-hand edge.
16. With a hot iron, press the direction of the long, center flanges in a random way to achieve a rumpled look to your quilt. Do this by manipulating and pulling the flange open along the fold and pressing flat (the flanges will become wrinkled to add interest). Repeat this pressing technique on each long, center flange the entire length of the quilt, from top to bottom.

17. Next, manipulate and press the 12" [30.5 cm] left and right flange sections of the Quilt Top downward toward the brown solid on the outside edges of the Quilt Top. Pull the batting and Quilt Back away from the Quilt Top and pin the manipulated flanges on the Quilt Top in place. Sew a ⅛" [3 mm] seam along the pinned sides to tack the flange edges in place, then smooth the edge of the Quilt Top back onto the batting and the Quilt Back to prepare for finishing the quilt edges.

FINISHING THE QUILT EDGES

18. Referring to the Fold Finish Edge instructions (page 28), trim the Quilt Back and the batting, then fold and pin the edges according to the directions.
19. Using the Double Stitch Edge (page 29), sew around the perimeter to finish the quilt.

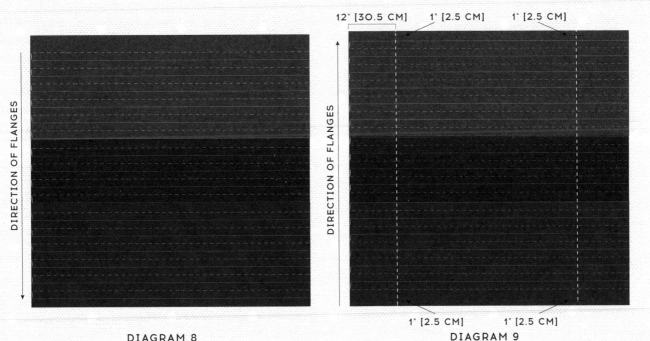

DIAGRAM 8

DIAGRAM 9

ENGLISH CROSS QUILT

FINISHED QUILT SIZE
72" x 72" [183 x 183 cm]

FINISHED CROSS SIZE
Approximately 18" x 18"
[46 x 46 cm]

HOW TOUGH?
●●●●●

Somewhat based on the flag of England, the English Cross Quilt actually has some Navajo influence, as well as a whisper of American folk art. The design is what I like to call "wonky," in that it's not symmetrical despite its geometric form. That's a big part of what gives this quilt its great character. This quilt is hard to mess up because its design is based on a very rough layout, but it'll take a little bit of time to cut and sew the crosses and piece together the stripes.

FABRICS AND SUPPLIES

- 2¼ yards [2 m] red print utility canvas for the Quilt Top
- 2¼ yards [2 m] ivory solid cotton linen for the Quilt Top
- 2¼ yards [2 m] brown print cotton linen for the Quilt Top
- 2¼ yards [2 m] brown solid broadcloth for the appliqué
- 2⅔ yards [2.5 m] rust solid for the appliqué
- 6⅛ yards [5.6 m] navy cotton linen for the appliqué and backing
- 4⅝ yards [4.3 m] ivory flannel for the batting
- 1⅔ yards [1.6 m] paper-backed fusible web
- Coordinating thread for piecing
- Coordinating spools of thread for machine appliqué in brown, rust, and navy

ADDITIONAL TOOLS

SEE BASIC TOOLS, PAGE 9
- Sewing-machine needle for heavyweight fabrics
- Basting spray
- Hand-sewing needle

FABRIC CUTTING INSTRUCTIONS

From the red print canvas x length of fabric (LOF), cut:
- Two A rectangles, 7" x 73" [17 x 185 cm]
- One B rectangle, 13½" x 73 " [34 x 185 cm]

From the ivory cotton linen x LOF, cut:
- One C rectangle, 4½" x 73" [11 x 185 cm]
- One D rectangle, 5" x 73 " [12 x 185 cm]
- Three E rectangles, 6" x 73 " [15 x 185 cm]
- One F rectangle, 8" x 73" [20 x 185 cm]

From the brown print cotton linen x LOF, cut:
- Four G rectangles, 5½" x 73" [14 x 185 cm]

From the brown broadcloth x LOF, cut:
- Nine H rectangles, 1½" x 73" [4 x 185 cm]

From the rust solid, cut:
- Nine strips, 7½" [19 cm] x width of fabric (WOF). From the strips, cut:
  > Eighteen I rectangles, 7½" x 18½" [19 x 47 cm]
  > Nine strips, 2¼" [5.5 cm] x WOF. From the strips, cut:
    > Eighteen J rectangles, 2¼" x 13½" [5.5 x 34 cm]

From the navy cotton linen, cut:
- Nine strips, 4½" [11 cm] x WOF. From the strips, cut:
  > Eighteen K rectangles, 4½" x 15½" [11 x 39 cm]

From the ivory flannel and the remaining navy linen fabrics, cut each into two equal lengths; trim off the selvage edges and set aside.

ASSEMBLE THE QUILT TOP

1. Referring to the order given in Diagram 1, sew the A through G rectangles together using a ½" [12 mm] seam allowance to complete the 73" x 73" [185 x 185 cm] Quilt Top; press the seam allowances toward the darker fabrics.

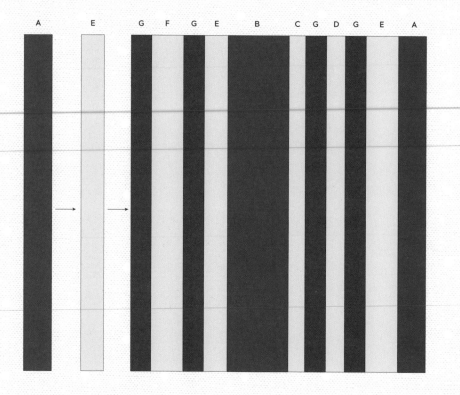

QUILT TOP

MAKE 1

DIAGRAM 1

APPLIQUÉ

2. Referring to Diagram 2 and using a polyester setting on your iron, lay one brown broadcloth H rectangle, **wrong** side up, on the ironing board. Fold both raw edges in to meet at the center of the strip and press in place along the entire length to make a finished ¾" x 73" [2 x 185 cm] H strip for Machine Appliqué (page 31). Make nine total. Flip the H strips over, with **right** sides facing up. Pin the strips to the red print A and B rectangles on the Quilt Top as shown, then top-stitch each strip lengthwise approximately 1/16" [2 mm] from both folded edges to secure to the Quilt Top.

   NOTE: *The technique used to create the crosses is not exact; wonky appliqué patches are the desired outcome.*

3. Referring to Diagram 3 (see page 138), select one rust solid I rectangle and lay it on the ironing board, **wrong** side up. Using your iron's cotton setting, fold in each corner ½" [12 mm] at a 45-degree angle and press. Then, in a wonky manner, fold over and press all four sides of your rectangle approximately ¼" [6 mm], to miter the corners. Please don't be concerned if they're not meeting exactly. With your scissors or a ruler and rotary cutter and mat, cut ⅜" [1 cm] wide strips of the paper-backed fusible web. Apply one strip along each folded edge of the I rectangle according to the manufacturer's instructions, preparing to fuse the rectangle to the Quilt Top. Follow the same steps to prepare the navy K rectangles and rust J rectangles. Make a total of eighteen each.

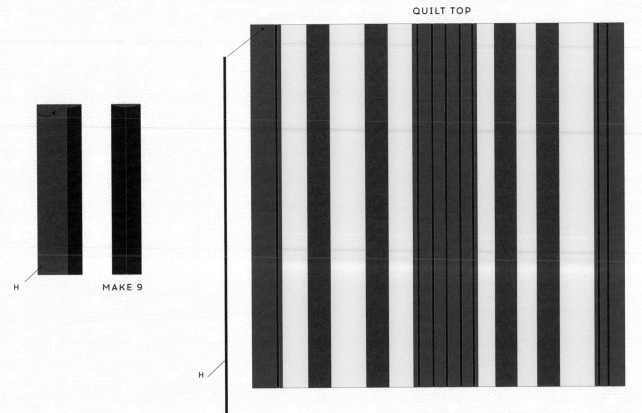

H   MAKE 9

H

QUILT TOP

DIAGRAM 2

4. Select two I rectangles and remove the paper backing from the fusible web strips. In the upper right corner of the Quilt Top, position the rectangles as shown in the top left of Diagram 4.
NOTE: *The placement of the crosses does not have to be perfect. A wonky placement lends charm to your finished quilt.*

5. Once satisfied with the position of the cross, remove the top, vertical rectangle, then press and fuse the bottom, horizontal rectangle in place according to the manufacturer's instructions. Next, topstitch ⅛" [3 mm] around the folded edges of the rectangle to secure it to the Quilt Top; backstitch at the starting and ending points and at each corner.

6. At the back of the appliquéd I rectangle, carefully trim away the Quilt Top fabric to within ⅜" [1 cm] of the appliqué stitch; discard the trimmed fabric piece.

7. Replace the second I rectangle vertically on top of the first appliquéd rectangle and press in place. Sew in place, then cut the bulk of the Quilt Top at the back as you did in Step 6. Referring to Diagram 4, continue adding rectangles to make nine large rust appliqué crosses.

8. Layer navy K rectangles in a cross-like manner on top of the large rust crosses and, in a similar manner, repeat Steps 5 to 7. Finally, layer, appliqué, and trim from the back of the J rectangles to finish the crosses and complete the Quilt Top.

PREP FOR QUILTING

9. Sew the two lengths of ivory flannel together lengthwise to use for the batting. In the same manner, sew the two lengths of navy linen together to use for the Quilt Back. Press the seams open.

10. Prepare the Quilt Top, batting, and the Quilt Back for quilting, according to Layering a Quilt Sandwich (page 22). Spray Baste (page 23) the Quilt Sandwich layers together.

MAKE 18

MAKE 18

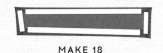

MAKE 18

DIAGRAM 3

QUILTING METHOD

11. Start and stop all quilting stitches 2" to 3" [5 to 7.5 cm] from the outside edges of the Quilt Top. First Stitch-in-the-Ditch (page 26) all of the visible, vertical seams of the red, ivory, and brown prints and brown solid strips.

12. Machine Shadow Stitch (page 25) around the perimeter of the small rust crosses ¼" [6 mm] from the outside edge, using navy thread to finish.

FINISHING THE QUILT EDGES

13. Trim the Quilt Back and the batting even with the Quilt Top, then refer to the Fold Finish Edge (page 28); trim the batting as instructed, then fold and pin the edges according to the directions.

14. Using a coordinating thread and a Double Stitch Edge (page 29), sew around the perimeter of the quilt. Go back and finish the Stitch-in-the-Ditch stitching you did in Step 11 to complete the quilt.

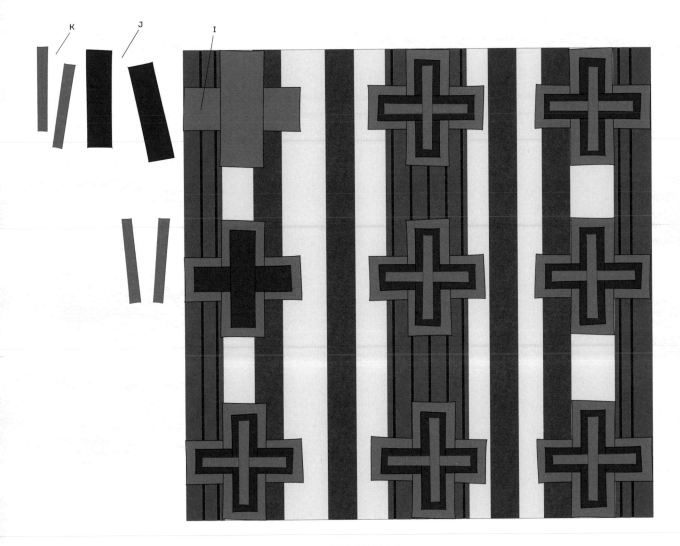

DIAGRAM 4

SOUTHWEST PASSAGE QUILT

FINISHED QUILT SIZE
72" x 72" [183 x 183 cm]

HOW TOUGH?
●●●●●

The beautifully folksy design of the Southwest Passage Quilt was borrowed from a Navajo weaving. I reinterpreted the basic structure to work within a quilt, and the design here still gives the quilt its off-kilter feel, but it is really doable without giving you too much anxiety. The hardest part about many of these quilts and their techniques are the imperfections! When things don't line up, it can be trickier than when they do.

FABRICS AND SUPPLIES

- 4¼ yards [3.9 m] rust solid for the Quilt Top
- 1⅜ yards [1.25 m] black solid for the appliqué
- 1⅔ yards [1.6 m] ivory solid for the appliqué
- 4⅝ yards [4.3 m] ivory flannel for the batting
- 4⅝ yards [4.3 m] of coordinating fabric for backing
- 1⅔ yards [1.6 m] paper-backed fusible web
- Coordinating spools of thread for machine appliqué in rust, ivory, and black

ADDITIONAL TOOLS

SEE BASIC TOOLS, PAGE 9
- Marking pencil
- One sheet of poster board, 22" x 28" [55 x 70 cm]
- Basting spray

TEMPLATE CUTTING INSTRUCTIONS

Cut the following templates from the template sheet enclosed in the envelope at the front of this book. Trace templates onto poster board and label each template (front and back), including seam allowances and grain lines; cut templates from poster board and set aside:
- Southwest Passage Template 1*
- Southwest Passage Template 2*

*Flip template vertically (long way) for the reverse side of the template and label it (1r or 2r, accordingly); include seam allowances and grain lines.

FABRIC CUTTING INSTRUCTIONS

From the rust solid, cut:
- Two lengths, 73" [185 cm] x width of fabric (WOF)

From the black solid, cut:
- Eight Template 1
- Eight Template 1r**
- Approximate sizes for tips of crosses as follows:
  - Twenty J rectangles, 1½" x 1¾" [4 x 4.5 cm]
  - Twenty-four K rectangles, 1¾" x 2" [4.5 x 5 cm]
  - Eight L rectangles, 1"x 2¼" [2.5 x 5.5 cm]

From the ivory solid, cut:
- Eight Template 2
- Eight Template 2r**
- Approximate sizes for crosses as follows:
  - Five A rectangles, 1½" x 11½" [4 x 29 cm]
  - Four B rectangles, 1½" x 29½" [4 x 75 cm]
  - One C rectangle, 1½" x 15½" [4 x 39 cm]
  - Two D rectangles, 1¾" x 5½" [4.5 x 14 cm]
  - Two E rectangles, 2" x 13½" [5 x 34 cm]
  - Two F rectangles, 1¾" x 7½" [4.5 x 19 cm]
  - Two G rectangles, 2¼" x 8" [5.5 x 20 cm]
  - Four H rectangles, 1¾" x 4½" [4.5 x 11 cm]
  - Four I rectangles, 2¼" x 5½" [5.5 x 14 cm]

From the ivory flannel and the coordinating backing yardages, cut each into two equal lengths; trim off the selvage edges and set aside.

r** = vertical reverse side of template

ASSEMBLE THE QUILT TOP

1. Sew the two rust solid 73" [185 cm] lengths together lengthwise using a ½" [12 mm] seam allowance; press to one side. Using coordinating thread, sew a Double Topstitch Seam (page 25) on the right side along and through the seam allowance to complete the Quilt Top base. Keeping the vertical topstitched seam centered, trim the Quilt Top base to 73" x 73" [185 x 185 cm].

APPLIQUÉ

NOTE: *The technique used to create the zigzag strips and crosses is not exact; wonky appliqué patches are the desired outcome.*

2. Referring to Diagram 1, select one ivory solid A rectangle and lay it on an ironing board, **wrong** side facing up. Using your iron's cotton setting, fold in the corners ½" [12 mm] at a 45-degree angle and press. In a wonky manner, fold in and press all four sides of the rectangle approximately ¼" [6 mm], making mitered corners. Don't be concerned if they're not meeting exactly. With your scissors or a ruler and rotary cutter with a cutting mat, cut ⅜" [1 cm] wide strips of paper-backed fusible web. Apply the strips along each edge of the ivory A rectangle according to the manufacturer's instructions. Make five rectangles total. In the same manner, prepare ivory B through I rectangles, black solid J and L rectangles, and all fabric pieces cut from Templates 1, 1r, 2, and 2r.

3. Fold and finger press the Quilt Top base in half both ways. Referring to Diagram 2 and working on a Design Wall (page 164) or other flat surface, remove the paper backing from the fusible web strips; lay out and pin all of the prepared black solid and ivory solid Templates 1, 1r, 2, and 2r on the Quilt Top base, using the finger-pressed folds as a guide. Unpin a prepared piece and then fuse it to the Quilt Top. Topstitch it in place with coordinating thread, a scant ⅛" [3 mm] from the folded edge. Topstitch around the entire edge to secure it to the Quilt Top base, backstitching at the starting and ending points and at each corner. Continue with this same process until all of the ivory and black fabric pieces are sewn in place.

4. Again referring to Diagram 2, and in the same manner as Step 3, remove the paper backing from the remaining ivory cross strips and black cross tips. Pin them in place, one cross at a time, and then fuse and topstitch each piece to secure it to the Quilt Top base. Secure each cross before moving on to the next one, until finished.

PREP FOR QUILTING

5. Sew the two lengths of ivory flannel together lengthwise to use for the batting. In the same manner, sew the two lengths of backing fabric together to use for the Quilt Back. Press the seams open.

6. Prepare your Quilt Back, batting, and Quilt Top for quilting, according to Layering a Quilt Sandwich (page 22). Spray Baste (page 23) the Quilt Sandwich layers together.

QUILTING METHOD

7. Using rust thread, machine Shadow Stitch (page 25) all zigzags and crosses ¼" [6 mm].

FINISHING THE QUILT EDGES

8. Referring to the Fold Finish Edge instructions (page 28), trim the Quilt Back and the batting, then fold and pin the edges according to the instructions.

9. Again using rust thread and a Double Stitch Edge (page 29), sew around the outside perimeter to finish the quilt.

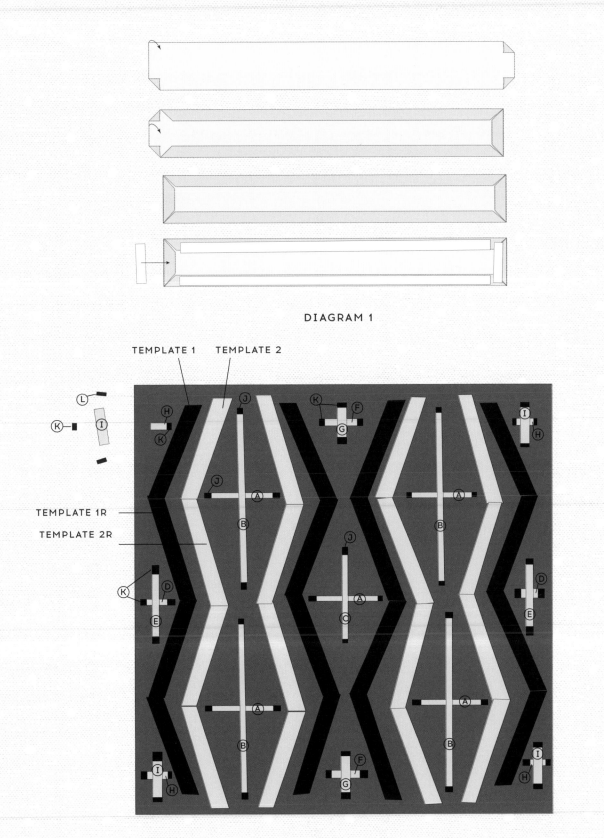

DIAGRAM 1

DIAGRAM 2

BULL'S-EYE QUILT

FINISHED QUILT SIZE
64" x 64" [163 x 163 cm]

HOW TOUGH?
●●●●●

This was my very first quilt design, created to promote my very first fabric line. It has also become my most popular design and, as a result, I felt compelled to include it in this book. The design, based on the R.A.F. roundel used to identify airplanes of the British Empire, was later adopted by mod (modern) bands of the 1960s such as The Who. I reinterpreted the design to include "pie slices" that give it a more "dartboard" look. The cutting and sewing of the round edges can be tricky for some, and it's a little less forgiving of those endearing mistakes than the other quilts.

FABRICS AND SUPPLIES

- ⅓ yard [0.3 m] each of four assorted green prints for blocks
- ⅜ yard [0.4 m] each of four assorted ivory prints for blocks
- ½ yard [0.5 m] each of four assorted blue prints for blocks
- 1 yard [1 m] each of four assorted black prints for blocks
- ⅜ yard [0.4 m] black print for binding
  NOTE: *We used one of the black prints used for the blocks as our binding, too.*
- 70" x 70" [175 x 175 cm] piece of cotton batting
- 4½ yards [4.2 m] of coordinating backing fabric

ADDITIONAL TOOLS

SEE BASIC TOOLS, PAGE 9
- One sheet of poster board, 22" x 28" [55 cm x 70 cm]
- Awl or small size circle paper punch
- Marking pencil
- Basting spray
- Curve Master Presser Foot for piecing curves; use according to manufacturer's instructions
- Design wall (optional)

TEMPLATE CUTTING INSTRUCTIONS

Cut the templates from the template sheet enclosed in the envelope at the front of this book. Trace the templates onto poster board and label each template, including seam allowances, match points, and grain lines; cut the templates from the poster board. Using an awl or paper punch, carefully poke a hole through the poster board template at each match point:

- Bull's Eye Template A
- Bull's Eye Template B
- Bull's Eye Template C
- Bull's Eye Template D

FABRIC CUTTING INSTRUCTIONS

Using a marking pencil, trace the templates and add match points onto the **wrong** side of each of the following fabrics:
- From each of four assorted green prints, cut two Template A
- From each of four assorted ivory prints, cut two Template B
- From each of four assorted blue prints, cut two Template C
- From each of two assorted black prints, cut two Template D
- From each of the remaining two assorted black prints, cut two Template Dr*
- From the ⅜ yard [0.4 m] black print, cut seven strips, 2½" [6 cm] x width of fabric (WOF); trim off the selvage edges and then set aside for binding.
- Cut the backing fabric into two equal lengths; trim off the selvage edges and set aside.

r* = reverse side of template

ASSEMBLE THE BLOCKS

NOTE: *Please install your Curve Master Presser Foot now and refer to the manufacturer's instructions before beginning to sew. See Diagram 1 for sewing order and for how blocks are pieced together.*

1. Select two identical green print A fabrics, two identical ivory print B fabrics, two identical blue print C fabrics, and two identical black print D fabrics. With right sides together and lining up match points along the curves, sew one green print A fabric to one ivory print B fabric. Press the seam open for A/B unit.
2. In the same manner, sew A/B unit to one blue print C fabric; press the seam open.
3. Sew A/B/C unit to one black print D fabric; press the seam open to complete the unit. Make two matching A/B/C/D units.
4. Repeat Steps 1 to 3 for two more matching A/B/C/D units.
5. Repeat Steps 1 to 3 to make two matching A/B/C/Dr units.

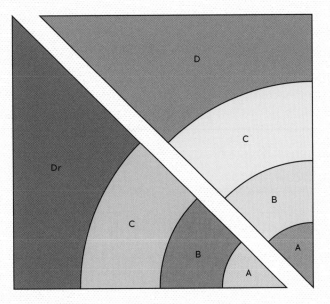

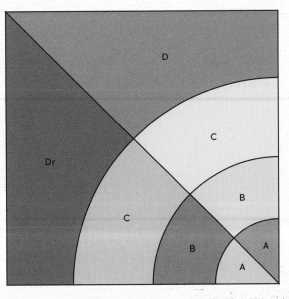

MAKE 2 SETS OF 2 MATCHING

DIAGRAM 1

6. With the remaining fabrics, make two more matching A/B/C/Dr units.
7. Paying attention to orientation, pin and sew together one A/B/C/D unit to one A/B/C/Dr unit to make one block. Make a second, identical block.
8. Repeat Step 6 with the remaining units for two more matching blocks.

ASSEMBLE THE QUILT TOP

9. Using a Design Wall (page 164) or other large, flat surface, lay out blocks referring to the flat image of the quilt (page 146). Sew the blocks into rows, pressing the seams open. Then sew rows together, pressing the seams open to finish your Quilt Top.

PREP FOR QUILTING

10. Sew the two lengths of backing fabric together to use for the Quilt Back. Press the seam open.
11. Prepare the Quilt Top, batting, and Quilt Back for quilting, according to Layering a Quilt Sandwich (page 22). Spray Baste (page 23) the layers together.

QUILTING METHOD

12. Referring to the Stitch-in-the-Ditch instructions (page 26), stitch along each of the seams, working from the center of the quilt out to the sides.

FINISHING THE QUILT EDGES

NOTE: *Referring to page 30, Self-Bind and follow these instructions.*

13. Make and attach the Double Fold Binding (page 26) using the black print 2½" [6 cm] strips.
14. If desired, use sandpaper to lightly sand along the surface areas and the outside edges of the Quilt Top to give a distressed look.

CARPETBAGGER QUILT

FINISHED QUILT SIZE
Approximately 77½" x 93½"
[197 x 237 cm]

HOW TOUGH?
● ● ● ● ●

The traditional folk block pattern, called Drunkard's Path, is the base of the Carpetbagger Quilt. There are several ways to use this versatile block pattern, but I love the basic contrast of the red and white in this one. Although this is probably the most traditional design in the book, it's also one of the most fun. Once you get into a rhythm making the blocks, you'll get a true sense of what quilting is all about. This one is only tough because of the scale and the difficulty of sewing on the curve.

GRITTY TECHNIQUES

LIGHT TEA STAINING: Follow the instructions on page 17 for use on ivory solid fabric to give the quilt a more antique look.

LIGHT SANDPAPER DISTRESSING: Follow the instructions on page 15 to distress the surface fabric and edges of the Quilt Top after the quilt is finished.

FABRICS AND SUPPLIES

- O 5½ yards [5.1 m] ivory solid for the blocks and the border
- O 6 yards [5.5 m] red solid for the blocks and the borders 1 and 3
- O 7½ yards [6.9 m] black solid for the backing and the self binding
- O 87" x 103" [221 x 262 cm] piece of cotton batting
- O Spool of 40 weight ivory cotton thread for piecing and quilting

ADDITIONAL TOOLS

SEE BASIC TOOLS, PAGE 9

- O One sheet of Quilter's Template, 22" x 28" [55 x 70 cm]
- O Awl
- O Marking pencil
- O Curve Master Presser Foot for piecing curves; use according to manufacturer's instructions
- O Basting spray
- O Design wall (optional)
- O Tools for tea staining (optional)
- O One sheet of coarse-grit sandpaper (optional)

TEMPLATE CUTTING INSTRUCTIONS

Using quilter's template plastic, trace the templates from the template sheet enclosed in the envelope at the front of this book. Label each template, including seam allowances, match points, and grain lines; cut templates from plastic. Using an awl, poke a hole through the template at each match point:

- O Carpetbagger Template A
- O Carpetbagger Template B

FABRIC CUTTING INSTRUCTIONS

NOTE: *If you are tea staining (page 17) the ivory fabric, be sure to perform this technique before cutting.*

From the ivory solid, cut:

- O Nine strips, 1½" [4 cm] x width of fabric (WOF). Sew the strips together to make:
  - › Two border strips, 1½" x 91" [4 x 231 cm]
  - › Two border strips, 1½" x 80" [4 x 203 cm]
  - › 336 pieces using Template A*
  - › 336 pieces using Template B*

From the red solid, cut:

- O Five strips, 1" [2.5 cm] x WOF. Sew the strips together to make:
  - › Two border strips, 1" x 89" [2.5 x 226 cm]
- O Four strips, 1¾" [4.5 cm] x WOF. Sew the strips together to make:
  - › Two border strips, 1¾" x 78" [4.5 x 198 cm]
- O Five strips, 1¼" [3 cm] x WOF. Sew the strips together to make:
  - › Two border strips, 1¼" x 93" [3.25 x 236 cm]
- O Four strips, 2½" [6 cm] x WOF. Sew the strips together to make:
  - › Two border strips, 2½" x 81" [6 x 206 cm]
- O 336 pieces using Template A*
- O 336 pieces using Template B*

Add match points to wrong side of fabric with marking pencil.

Cut the black solid yardage into three equal pieces; trim off the selvage edges and set aside.

ASSEMBLE THE BLOCKS

NOTE: *Please install your Curve Master Presser Foot now and refer to the manufacturer's instructions before beginning to sew. See diagrams for sewing order and for how blocks are pieced together.*

1. Referring to Diagram 1, with **right** sides together and ivory A on top, line up match points along the curves; sew to one red B. Press the seam allowance toward B to make one 3½" [9 cm] square. Make 336 squares in each colorway, pairing ivory A pieces with red B pieces and red A pieces with ivory B pieces.

2. Select eight squares of each colorway and lay them out into a Drunkard's Path block, as shown in Diagram 1. Piece the squares into rows, pressing every other row's seam allowances in opposite directions. Sew rows together and press the seam allowances to one side to make one block. Make forty-two blocks total.

BLOCK UNITS

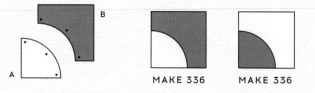

MAKE 336   MAKE 336

DRUNKARD'S PATH BLOCK

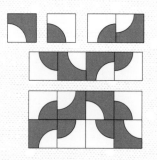 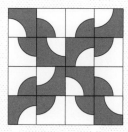

MAKE 42

DIAGRAM 1

ASSEMBLE THE QUILT TOP

3. Using a Design Wall (page 164) or other flat surface, lay out seven rows of six blocks according to Diagram 2. Sew the blocks into rows, pressing each row's seams in opposite directions. Sew rows together, pressing seams in one direction to make the center of your Quilt Top.

4. Sew the red 1" x 89" [2.5 x 226 cm] border strips to the sides of the quilt; press the seam allowances toward the red strips. Trim the excess strip length even with the top and bottom of the quilt center. Sew the red 1¾" x 78" [4.5 x 198 cm] border strips to the top and bottom of the quilt; press the seam allowances toward the red strips. Trim the excess length even with the sides of the quilt center to complete Border 1.

5. Sew the ivory 1½ x 91" [4 x 231 cm] border strips to the sides of the quilt; press the seam allowances toward the red strips. Trim the excess strip length even with the top and bottom of the quilt center and Border 1. Sew the ivory 1½" x 80" [4 x 203 cm] border strips to the top and bottom of the quilt; press the seam allowances toward the red strips. Trim the excess length even with the sides of the quilt center and Border 1 to complete Border 2.

6. Sew the red 1¼" x 93" [3 x 236 cm] border strips to the sides of the quilt; press the seam allowances toward the red strips. Trim the excess strip length even with the top and bottom of the quilt center and the Borders. Sew the red 2½" x 81" [6 x 206 cm] border strips to the top and bottom of the quilt; press the seam allowances toward the red border strips and trim the excess length even with the side borders of the quilt center for Border 3. This completes the Quilt Top. Set aside to assemble the batting and the Quilt Back.

PREP FOR QUILTING

7. Sew the three lengths of the black solid together to use for the Quilt Back. Press the seams open. The seams will run horizontally across the back of the quilt when layering the Quilt Sandwich.

8. Prepare the Quilt Back, batting, and Quilt Top for quilting, according to Layering a Quilt Sandwich (page 22). Spray Baste (page 23) the Quilt Sandwich layers together.

QUILTING METHOD

9. Use the Stitch-in-the-Ditch (page 26) method of quilting along all seams of the Quilt Top.

FINISHING THE QUILT EDGES

10. Pull the backing out of the way and trim the batting even with the edge of the Quilt Top. Next, trim the backing fabric so it's 1¼" [3 cm] larger than the Quilt Top/batting on all four sides.

11. Self Bind (page 30) the quilt with backing fabric to complete the quilt.

12. If desired, use sandpaper to lightly sand along the surface areas and outside edges of the Quilt Top to give the quilt a more distressed look.

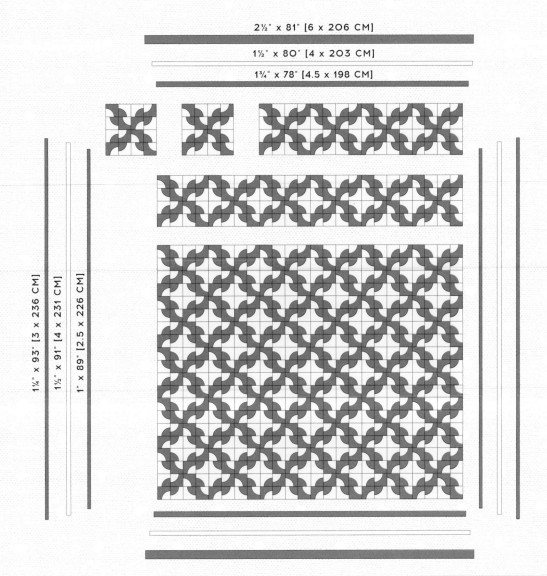

DIAGRAM 2

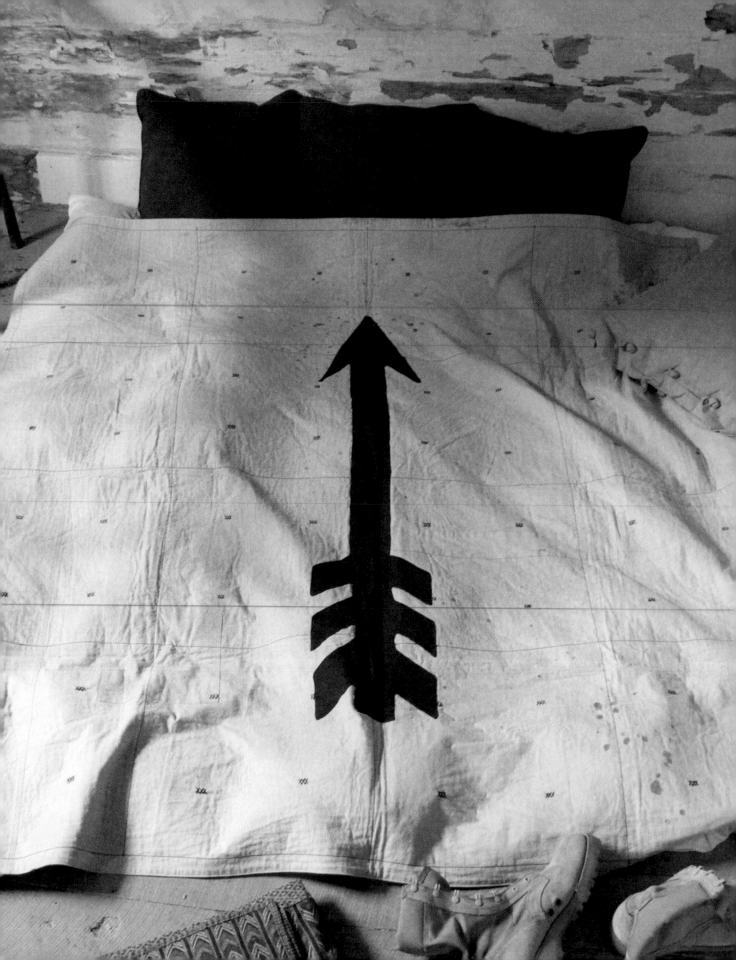

ARROW QUILT

FINISHED QUILT SIZE
72" x 72" [183 x 183 cm]

HOW TOUGH?
●●●●●

The simple design of the Arrow Quilt belies a tactile patchwork of rugged piecing. I gave it a 5 on the toughness scale because of working with the thickness of the denim fabric as an appliqué, but a newer quilter could use a Raw Edge Appliqué (page 31) for an easier go at it. Blocks of my coffee- and oil-stained white heavy cotton duck are patched together and finished off with the arrow in black cotton. The use of the Triple-X Hand Stitch (page 24) creates a very eclectic and raw-looking finished design. It seems to be one of the guys' favorites—at least the guys I hang out with.

GRITTY TECHNIQUES

HEAVY COFFEE STAINING: Follow the instructions on page 17 to use on the muslin before cutting into the fabric. This will give the muslin an antique look.

PAINT STAINING: After the coffee staining, you can follow the instructions on page 19 to add brown dyes or stains to areas of the muslin to give the appearance of stains from use. Apply any dyes or stains before cutting into the fabric.

HEAVY SANDPAPER DISTRESSING: Follow the instructions on page 15 to use on the Quilt Top surface and outside edges after it is completed to give it a worn look and feel.

FABRICS AND SUPPLIES

- O 4½ yards [4.2 m] muslin for the Quilt Top
- O 15" x 60" [38 x 153 cm] piece of dark blue denim for the appliqué arrow
- O 4¾ yards [4.4 m] ivory flannel for the batting
- O 4¾ yards [4.4 m] coordinating backing fabric
- O Coordinating spools of thread for machine appliqué in dark blue and ivory
- O Spool of dark gray cotton embroidery thread for quilting and tying

ADDITIONAL TOOLS

SEE BASIC TOOLS, PAGE 9
- O Tools for coffee staining (optional)
- O Paint/dyes for staining (optional)
- O Two sheets of poster board, 22" x 28" [55 x 70 cm]
- O Transparent tape
- O One roll of freezer paper
- O Marking pencil
- O Sewing-machine needle for heavyweight fabrics
- O Basting spray
- O Hand-embroidery needle
- O Large box of quilter's safety pins
- O Two sheets of medium-coarse grit sandpaper (optional)

TEMPLATE CUTTING INSTRUCTIONS

Cut the two Arrow Template pieces from the template sheet enclosed in the envelope at the front of this book. Trace the templates onto poster board and label the templates with grain lines, **right** side facing up. Cut the two template pieces from the poster board and use transparent tape to connect the two pieces where indicated to make the arrow. Next, trace the template again with the **right** side up onto the matte paper side of the freezer paper. Cut the arrow shape from the freezer paper and set aside.

FABRIC CUTTING INSTRUCTIONS

NOTE: *If you are staining or dyeing (page 19) the muslin, be sure to perform these techniques before cutting into the fabric.*

From the muslin, cut:
- Two strips, 73" [185 cm] x width of fabric (WOF)

From the remaining muslin, cut:
- Five random-size patches

From the ivory flannel and the backing yardage, cut each into two equal lengths; trim off selvage edges and set aside.

PREPARE FOR APPLIQUÉ

For this project we used the Freezer Paper Method of Appliqué (page 31) for a finished edge. For a simpler process, you may want to consider using Raw Edge Appliqué (page 31).

1. Lay the **right** side of the poster board Arrow Template onto the **wrong** side of the denim. Using a marking pencil or pen, trace the template onto the fabric; cut the arrow shape from the denim.

2. Lay the denim arrow along the length of your ironing board, **wrong** side up. Lay the freezer paper arrow shape on top of the denim with the wax side up. Begin poking straight pins around the edges of the freezer paper through the denim and ironing board padding to keep the freezer paper from shifting as you work.

3. Begin folding the denim seam allowance onto the freezer paper edge and, using caution, press the seam allowance with a hot iron to adhere the denim to the freezer paper; try not to touch the freezer paper with your iron. At the curved edges, snip through the seam allowance in a perpendicular manner to within a few threads from the traced pencil mark. This allows you to manipulate the fabric around curves for easier pressing. Set aside while you make the Quilt Top.

ASSEMBLE THE QUILT TOP

4. With the wrong sides together and using a ½" [12 mm] seam allowance, pin and sew the stained muslin lengths together; press the seam allowance to one side. Double Topstitch (page 25) along the seam vertically on the **right** side of the Quilt Top.

5. With the seam centered on the pieced muslin Quilt Top, trim the sides so the Quilt Top measures 73" [185 cm] square. Add the stained muslin patches randomly to the Quilt Top (see Diagram 1 for guide on placement) by turning and pressing the raw edges ¼" [6 mm]. Pin the patches in place, and appliqué them to the Quilt Top by using a Double Topstitch (page 25).

DIAGRAM 1

PREP FOR QUILTING

6. Sew the two lengths of ivory flannel together lengthwise to use for the batting. In the same manner, sew the two lengths of backing together to use for the Quilt Back. Press the seams open.

7. Prepare the Quilt Back, batting, and Quilt Top for quilting according to the Layering a Quilt Sandwich instructions on page 22, Spray Basting (page 23) the layers together.

QUILTING METHOD

8. Referring to the quilt image and using your ruler and a fabric marking pencil, lightly draw out a 17½" [44.5 cm] square grid on the muslin Quilt Top (the outside edge of the grid should measure 70" x 70" [178 x 178 cm]). Begin the grid 1" [2.5 cm] away from the finished edge measurement of the Quilt Top on all four sides.

9. Using dark gray machine embroidery thread, Straight Line Quilt (page 26) along the marked pencil grid lines.

10. With the Quilt Top seam positioned vertically, fold it in half horizontally and finger press along the fold. Open the Quilt Top. Fold the denim appliqué arrow in half, horizontally, and finger press. Remove the freezer paper from the back and center the **wrong** side of the arrow to the **right** side of the Quilt Top, along the horizontal finger-pressed fold of the muslin Quilt Top and vertical Double Topstitch Seam (see Step 4). Pin in place around the perimeter of the arrow's edge. Using dark blue thread, Machine Appliqué (page 31) the arrow to the Quilt Top, sewing a scant ⅛" [3 mm] from the arrow's edge.

11. Use a ruler and place a safety pin 3" [7.5 cm] in from each corner of a 17½" [44.5 cm] machine-quilted square through all layers. Repeat this for each square on the Quilt Top. There should be four safety pins in each square. Using a double strand of the dark gray embroidery thread, embroider a Triple-X Hand Stitch (page 24) at each safety pin to complete the quilting.

FINISHING THE QUILT EDGES

12. Referring to the Fold Finish Edge (page 28), trim the Quilt Back and batting, then fold and pin the edges according to the directions.

13. Using the ivory thread and a Double Stitch Edge (page 29), sew around the perimeter to finish the quilt.

14. If desired, use sandpaper to heavily distress the quilt along the seams and the outside edges of the Quilt Top to give the quilt a more distressed look.

GLOSSARY

APPLIQUÉ—A finished edge or raw edge surface embellishment made by cutting a single layer of fabric into a shape and then hand or machine stitching it to a base layer. See Appliqué Stitching on page 31.

BACKSTITCH—Doubling back on the beginning and/or ending of a row of stitches to strengthen and secure starting and ending points.

BASTE—Temporary, long running stitches created by hand or machine to hold fabric in place before quilting.

BASTING SPRAY—A tacky adhesive spray that temporarily holds two pieces of fabric together or the layers of a Quilt Sandwich together in place of hand- or machine-sewn basting stitches. Basting spray can be found at your local quilt shop or fabric retail chain.

BINDING—A strip of fabric used to cover and enclose the raw edges of the perimeter of a quilt.

BLANKET STITCH—A hand stitch, used for embellishing a fabric edge or finishing the edge of a quilt or blanket, eliminating unraveling.

BLOCK OR QUILT BLOCK—Pieces of cut fabric sewn together that typically make a square or rectangular unit. Units are then pieced together to make a Quilt Top.

BORO STYLE—A trend in textiles referring to the eighteenth- to nineteenth-century Japanese "method" of mending and patching fabrics with rags made of indigo-dyed cloth. See Quilting Methods on page 24.

CROSS STITCH—A stitch that is formed by two stitches crossing each other diagonally (see page 33).

DESIGN WALL—A vertical wall, wrapped with either flannel or quilt batting, where one can temporarily arrange and preview fabric patches, quilt blocks, or other patchwork before sewing. A design wall assists in the decision-making process of where the elements of a quilt look best.

DRAPE—The fluid way a fabric hangs.

FAT QUARTER—One quarter of a yard of fabric that measures 18" x 22" [46 x 56 cm]. Achieved by taking 1 yard [91 cm] of 44" [112 cm] wide fabric and making two cuts: first, cut the yard in half widthwise from selvage edge to selvage edge, giving you two half-yards. Then, cut each half-yard lengthwise (along the fold) for four fat quarters.

FEED SACK—Made from cotton prints, homespun, muslin, linen, or canvas fabric, feed sacks were and, in some cases, still are used by farmers to store and transport grain, feed, seeds, and flour. Feed sacks were hand sewn in the early days, then mass-produced in the late 1800s once the sewing machine was invented.

FINGER PRESS—The method of pressing a fold or a crease using the pressure from your fingers, as opposed to using an iron.

FREEZER PAPER—Paper that has a matte finish on one side and a wax finish on the other. Freezer paper is white in color and on a roll and can be found at your local grocery store. Quilters use freezer paper for a finished-edge appliqué technique.

FUSSY CUT—To center and cut a selected design from printed fabric, thereby giving the element a sense of importance.

GRAIN—The orientation of the threads in woven fabric: lengthwise and crosswise. The lengthwise grain is parallel to the selvage and is called the warp. Cross-grain threads are woven over and under the warp threads and are perpendicular to the selvage.

MATCH POINT—A point marked on one pattern piece for the purpose of matching a similar point marked on a second pattern piece, then pinning and sewing the pieces together.

PAPER-BACKED FUSIBLE WEB—Heat-sensitive adhesive webbing backed with paper, enabling one fabric to bind to another fabric. Refer to the manufacturer's instructions for proper application.

PATINA—The addition of character or visual interest to the surface of an object or item that naturally occurs over time; oxidation. Today's use of the word is rather broad and is defined here as a desired state achieved intentionally on the surface of a new object or item (such as through distressing cloth) to make it look old, adding character and a much-loved look.

PIVOT—A point where machine sewing stops with the needle still buried in the fabric, the presser foot is lifted, the fabric is rotated (typically 45 degrees), and sewing continues in a new direction.

PRESHRINK OR PREWASH—To wash and dry fabric before cutting or sewing.

PRESSER FOOT—Holds fabric in place with pressure on the bed of the sewing machine and works with the feed dogs to move the fabric as it is sewn.

QUILT—A coverlet used for warmth and/or decorative purposes consisting of three layers: a Quilt Top, batting, and backing (or Quilt Back), otherwise known as the Quilt Sandwich. The layers are stitched together to stabilize the quilt and to keep the layers from shifting. To *quilt a quilt*, or *quilting a quilt*, describes the action of sewing the Quilt Sandwich together.

RAW EDGE—An unfinished, cut edge of fabric.

RIGHT SIDE—The decorative, printed side, or top, finished side of cloth.

ROTARY CUTTER—A craft tool generally used by quilters consisting of a handle and a round blade that rotates to cut fabric. A rotary cutter is typically used along with a quilter's ruler and rotary cutting mat.

ROTARY CUTTING MAT—A self-healing surface used along with a rotary cutter to cut fabric. The mat prevents damage to a work surface and helps maintain the rotary cutter blade's sharpness.

RUNNING STITCH—A straight, hand-sewn stitch that weaves in and out of the fabric, resulting in a dashed line. In quilting, a running stitch can be used to baste the Quilt Sandwich before beginning the quilting process.

SEAM—The joined point of two or more layers of fabric held together using hand or machine stitches.

SEAM ALLOWANCE—The distance between the stitching line and the cut edge of your fabric. In quilting, the measurement is conventionally ¼" [6 mm], but may be as large as ½" [12 mm] when sewing with heavy-weight fabrics.

SELVAGE—Tightly woven factory edge of fabric that runs parallel to the lengthwise grain, or warp, stabilizing and preventing yardage from unraveling.

SLIPSTITCH—Frequently used to join two folded edges, slipstitching is nearly invisible, as the thread is slipped under the fabric's fold. You'll need a long piece of thread and a sharp needle.

A. To begin, feed one end of the thread through the eye of the needle, doubling the thread back on itself. Match the cut ends and make a double knot.

B. Insert your needle into one piece of fabric, at the folded edge, coming up from the **wrong** side, and pull the thread taut, hiding the knot.

C. Then insert the needle through a few threads on the other edge of the fabric. Pull the thread through until it is taut.

D. Insert the needle back into the first side, through about ½" [12 mm] of the fabric, hiding the thread inside the fold. Push the needle through the fabric and again pull the thread taut.

E. Repeat this process until you have stitched your fabric together, keeping even spaces between stitches.

F. To finish, tie off your stitching by making a double knot close to the fabric and cut the extra thread.

SLOPPY EMBROIDERY—Hand-sewing an embroidery stitch that is not perfectly executed; stitches are uneven and sloppy, bringing a quirky sort of charm to the Quilt Top.

SQUARE UP—Trimming away excess fabric, such as from a quilt block or Quilt Top, to make the edges uniform and the corners into right angles before continuing with the next step.

STITCH LENGTH—Length of a stitch determined by the movement of the feed dogs (machine sewing).

STITCH-IN-THE-DITCH—Stitching inside the "valley" or "groove" of a Quilt Top's seam through all three layers of the Quilt Sandwich.

STRAIGHT STITCH—The most basic machine stitch, producing a single row of straight, even stitches.

TOPSTITCH—Stitching two or more layers of fabric together when constructing the Quilt Top or piecing backing together.

WALKING FOOT—A presser foot that works like the feed dogs by gripping and moving the fabric to facilitate even feed.

WHIP STITCH—A series of stitches that flow over the edge of two pieces of fabric or two folds of fabric, joining them together for a finished edge.

WONKY—Crooked; askew.

WRONG SIDE—The unprinted or back of printed cloth.

YARDAGE—A general term to describe the length of fabric cut from a bolt and measured in yards/meters or fractions of yards/meters.

INDEX

A

Appliqué, 31, 164
Arrow Quilt, 158–63

B

Backing, 22
Back Stitch, 32, 164
Baking fabric, 17
Basting
 definition of, 164
 methods, 23
 spray, 164
Batting, 22
Bear Paw Quilt, 88–93
Binding, 164
Blanket Stitch, 32, 164
Block, 164
Boro Stitch, 33
Boro style, 119, 164
Bull's-Eye Quilt, 146–51

C

Canvas
 characteristics of, 12
 distressing, 15
Carpetbagger Quilt, 152–57
Coal Mine Quilt, 118–23
Coffee staining, 17
Cotton
 characteristics of, 12
 distressing, 15
Cross Stitch, 33, 164

D

Denim
 characteristics of, 12
 distressing, 15
Design wall, 164
Diagonal Straight Line
 Quilting, 26
Distressing, 13, 15, 35
Double Fold Binding, 26–27
Double Stitch Edge, 29
Double Topstitch Seam, 25
Double-X Stitch, 24, 33
Drape, 164
Drunkard's Path pattern, 153
Duck canvas, 12
Dyeing
 indigo, 19
 rough, 19
 tools for, 16

E

1890s Trader's Quilt, 82–87

Embroidery
 sloppy, 165
 stitches, 32–33
English Cross Quilt, 132–39

F

Fabrics
 baking, 17
 canvas, 12
 choosing, 11
 cotton, 12
 denim, 12
 distressing, 13, 15, 35
 dyeing, 19
 fading, 16, 18
 linen, 12
 prepping, 8
 staining, 16–19
 vintage, 13
 width of, 8
 wool, 12
Fading, 16, 18
Falling Wind Quilt, 124–31
Fat quarter, 164
Feed sack, 164
Finger press, 164
Fold Finish Edge, 28–29
Forged Block Quilt, 50–53
Fort Battery Quilt, 74–81
Freezer Paper Appliqué, 31,
 164
Fusible web, paper-backed,
 164–65
Fussy cut, 164

G

Grain, 164
Grainery Quilt, 40–45

H

Hand stitching, 24
Horse Blanket Quilt, 62–67

I

Indigo dyeing, 19
Iron Bars Quilt, 46–49

L

Linen
 characteristics of, 12
 distressing, 15

M

Machine Appliqué, 31
Machine quilting, 25–26
Maritime Quilt, 54–61
Match point, 164
Modified Blanket Stitch, 32

N

Navajo Blanket Quilt, 36–39

O

Old Glory Quilt, 68–73

P

Painted Desert Quilt, 108–17
Patina, 165
Pivot, 165
Preshrinking, 165
Presser foot, 165
Prewashing, 165

Q

Quilt back, 22
Quilt block, 164
Quilt edges, finishing, 26–30
Quilting
 hand stitching, 24
 machine, 25–26
 prep for, 22
Quilts
 Arrow Quilt, 158–63
 Bear Paw Quilt, 88–93
 Bull's-Eye Quilt, 146–51
 Carpetbagger Quilt,
  152–57
 Coal Mine Quilt, 118–23
 definition of, 165
 1890s Trader's Quilt,
  82–87
 English Cross Quilt,
  132–39
 Falling Wind Quilt,
  124–31
 Forged Block Quilt, 50–53
 Fort Battery Quilt, 74–81
 Grainery Quilt, 40–45
 Horse Blanket Quilt,
  62–67
 Iron Bars Quilt, 46–49
 Maritime Quilt, 54–61
 Navajo Blanket Quilt,
  36–39
 Old Glory Quilt, 68–73
 Painted Desert Quilt,
  108–17
 Skeleton Crew Quilt,
  102–7
 Southwest Passage Quilt,
  140–45
 World's Fair Quilt, 94–101
Quilt sandwich, layering, 22
Quilt top, 22

R

Raw edge, definition of, 165
Raw Edge Appliqué, 31
Right side, 165
Rotary cutter, 165
Rotary cutting mat, 165
Rough dyeing, 19
Running Stitch, 33, 165

S

Safety Pin Basting, 23
Seam
 allowance, 8, 165
 definition of, 165
 Double Topstitch, 25
Self-Binding, 30
Selvage, 165
Shadow Stitching, 25
Single Stitch Edge, 29
Skeleton Crew Quilt, 102–7
Slipstitch, 165
Sloppy embroidery, 165
Southwest Passage Quilt,
 140–45
Spray Basting, 23
Square up, 166
Staining
 baking fabric after, 17
 coffee, 17
 natural, 18
 tea, 17
 tools for, 16
Stitch-in-the-Ditch, 26, 166
Stitch length, 166
Straight Line Quilting, 26
Straight Stitch, 166

T

Tea staining, 17
Thread Basting, 23
Tools, 9
Topstitch, 166
Triple-X Stitch, 24, 33
Tying the quilt, 24

V

Vintage fabrics, 13

W

Walking foot, 166
Whip Stitch, 166
Wonky, definition of, 166
Wool, 12
World's Fair Quilt, 94–101
Wrong side, 166

X

X-Edge Stitch, 29, 33

Y

Yardage, 166